SUBURBAN BOY

Growing up in
South-East London
in the 1930s

ADRIAN BRISTOW

THE HISTORY PRESS

First published in the United Kingdom in 2008 by
The History Press
The Mill • Brimscombe Port • Stroud • Gloucestershire • GL5 2QG

British Library Cataloguing in Publication Data
A catalogue record for this book is available from the British Library.

ISBN 978-07509-5035-0

Typeset in 11/13.5pt Sabon
Typesetting and origination by
The History Press.
Printed and bound in England.

CONTENTS

	Introduction	v
One	Boundaries	1
Two	Parents & Relations	7
Three	Auntie Walters	17
Four	Early Days & Army Ways	25
Five	A Mixed Infant	34
Six	House & Garden	41
Seven	Close Relatives; Closet Relations	48
Eight	Under Taurus	56
Nine	Balls & Wheels	66
Ten	Parks & Commons	75
Eleven	Collectables	81
Twelve	Sea & Sand	88
Thirteen	Jaunts & Jollities	97
Fourteen	Sacred & Profane	103
Fifteen	Evening Entertainments	111
Sixteen	In a Large Pond	119
Seventeen	Transports of Delight	126
Eighteen	The Wine Press	132
Nineteen	Growing Pains	137
Twenty	The End of the Beginning	142
	Epilogue	147

'Is this bilge,' he asked, 'to be printed?'
'Privately. It will be placed in the family archives for the benefit of my grandchildren.'

Laughing Gas, P.G. Wodehouse

INTRODUCTION

'Bow, Bow, ye lower-middle classes!
Bow, Bow, ye tradesmen, bow ye masses!'
Iolanthe, W.S. Gilbert

I am a child of my time, and that time, though I can hardly believe it, is now over seventy years ago. I was brought up in Woolwich, a suburb of London, in the 1930s and I have tried to conjure up what it was like for a boy growing up in a specific stratum of society, a lower-middle-class home, at that time. So my book may be seen as something of a postcard of a vanished age from a boy's perspective. A vanished age indeed! The landscape, the buildings and the parks I remember are still mostly there but the people have gone, their pre-war way of life has altered dramatically, and the nature of the boyhood I enjoyed has disappeared forever.

The momentous events of the 1930s – the Depression, the abdication, the rise of Hitler and the coming of war in 1939 – formed the background to a boyhood which I never thought of as anything other than unremarkable. But, looking back, it now seems quite remarkable in many aspects. Before the memory of the vivid scenes, figures and places of my early years fades, it is the matter-of-fact nature of my childhood that I wish to convey. Fortunately, many people who lived through that decade are still alive and I hope this memoir, particularly the humdrum domestic and social detail, may awaken echoes of a half-forgotten yet treasured past. For my younger readers – well, those under seventy – if distance does not exactly lend enchantment, then perhaps it might arouse a certain curiosity about the way many of us lived then.

At present, recollections of childhood before and during the Second World War have rarely been so popular. Everywhere, gates to the secret gardens of memory stand unlatched and articles and slim volumes of early times remembered rattle from the presses. They seem to be of two types. There are reminiscences of childhoods spent in tranquil villages under the downs, with memories of golden days in great houses and of timeless afternoons bathed in sunshine. Sturdy little figures in pinafore dresses and floppy white hats stump across buttercup meadows to the brook; small boys and large trunks are dispatched by steam to unbearable prep schools. And all the while, the grandfather clock in the echoing hall ticks off the hours of childhood.

The other kind reveals, in uncompromising detail, grim tales of childhoods between the wars among northern back-to-backs or the decaying tenements of the capital. Here, amid poverty of mind and pocket, and draining unemployment, life is punctuated by sordid dramas played out in squalid kitchens. Often the only redeeming feature is the figure of Ma or Mam, monumental among the ruins. It's all good material, of course, for the inevitable first novel. My recollections, however, are of a different kind, for, as far as I can discover, there are few memoirs dedicated to growing up in an essentially lower-middle-class home in London during the 1930s.

I should like to stress that my family was undeniably lower-middle class, though of recent working-class origin. My father was not a manual worker or a skilled craftsman, but essentially a clerk, a white-collar worker, whose wife did not go out to work, even part-time. He was part of that upwardly-mobile movement of future owner-occupiers (via the building societies), some of whose children were to become first-generation grammar school pupils and university graduates. Such families (I am generalising now) were respectable, respectful, conformist, mainly conservative, patriotic, class-conscious and not overly concerned about religion. And, if some of those characteristics happened to be shared with the middle-class, so much the better for unspoken aspirations. Consciousness of class lay heavily upon the lower-middle classes and our lives were shaped in insidious ways by its subtleties. I make no apology for emphasising this because it was a major factor in social life.

I realise that for most adults under seventy, the 1930s are as remote, funny, savage and inexplicable as the Edwardian era of my parents was to me. To them, the 1930s means, essentially, the Depression, with mass unemployment and the rise of Hitler – and not much else. This view of the decade appears deeply embedded in the popular mind and has been created over the years partly by folk memories of the past and partly by contemporary newsreels, newspapers, television documentaries and political rhetoric. Because some would consider my childhood was spent against a tawdry backcloth, perhaps I might be allowed to enter one major caveat. The grinding poverty and despair caused by mass unemployment that characterised large areas of the country did not extend, by and large, to the south of England. I saw virtually nothing of the effects of the slump in my part of London, or where we travelled in Kent and Sussex, but I was, after all, only a young boy, fully occupied with my microscopic affairs. In fact, for many it was a time of rising living standards, while the country continued to enjoy a prolonged period of social peace. There was relatively little crime against either person or property, and people remained law-abiding, tolerant and deferential. There also existed a proud sense of national identity, buttressed by victory in war (though achieved at grievous cost in life) and enhanced by a still extensive empire.

I was fortunate; but I was not exceptional in this. Most of my friends spent happy childhoods in close-knit families in modest houses. There was always enough to eat and we were properly dressed and shod. Our parents played for hours with us at home, and showed us the wonders of London on days out. They introduced us to castles and cathedrals during our summer holiday at the seaside; the summers in the 1930s were long, warm and sunny – *vide Wisden passim*. We had strong, if slightly bemused, support at school, though there was no question then of parents becoming involved in our schools or actually visiting them. Apart from taking us to the mixed infant departments when we first started and collecting us later in the day, contact stopped at the school gates. Pocket money was minimal but we can never remember, though hard-up, feeling hard done by. Ours was a small, intimate world of home, neighbourhood and school, with few clouds on our horizon.

In retrospect, there seems to have been a singular richness about my early years, although it was certainly not apparent at the time. The richness was derived partly from the loving web of relatives and quasi-relatives which enmeshed and protected me, and partly from a variety of experiences, many of which had vanished long before my own children were growing up. Thus my children and grandchildren know very little of the routines and domestic arrangements that dominated my life at school and at home. They are unaware of the interests that absorbed my seemingly endless leisure, or of the curious games and activities my friends and I pursued. Again, many of these pursuits have disappeared forever, while others seem hopelessly out-dated.

Two last comments. I realise that, like all children, I absorbed certain values, prejudices and attitudes from my parents and their contemporaries. Both my parents were born in 1896 and grew up in the Edwardian era and during the First World War. They were as much prisoners of their childhoods as I am of mine. Thus their childhood experiences inevitably affected my upbringing and coloured my life for some years. I have tried, not always successfully, to avoid making comparisons, either implicitly or explicitly, between then and now. Instead, I hope that my readers will draw their own conclusions without being buffeted about the head with the faded splendours of times past.

ONE

BOUNDARIES

'Forget the spreading of the hideous town;
Think rather of the pack horse on the down,
And dream of London, small and white, and clean,
The clear Thames bordered by its gardens green.'
Prologue, *The Earthly Paradise*, William Morris

Unlike most of those who write about their childhood, I cannot pretend to have either an accurate or a detailed memory. Certain incidents, some significant at the time, others of so little consequence I cannot understand why I should have remembered them, stand out vividly, but they do so against a blur of happy domestic activity. I cannot recall even fragmentary conversations from my early boyhood and it irritates me that I can no longer remember the exact details of some scenes I wish to recapture.

Luckily, I do have an accurate visual memory for people, landscape and townscape, for houses and streets, for shops and parks. I can conjure up in my mind's eye what people looked like and what they wore, helped here by a collection of old family snaps. A child of my time, I write the word 'snaps' automatically.

During the few years I am attempting to recall, characters move in and out of focus, and they grow or diminish in importance at certain stages. When one is young, familiar adults rarely alter or grow older, although some mysteriously vanish from the scene, either from natural causes or by courtesy of Pickfords. It is usually the grandparents, the 'nanas' and 'grandpas', or elderly friends of the family, who first bring awareness of death. Such losses, limited as they are in number and spread over several years, do not cause great sadness and are soon forgotten in the excitement of growing up.

I have tried to be as accurate and as honest as possible in my recollections. I am encouraged by the fact that as I write about my early years, as I exercise and rack my memory, incidents and details I had overlooked and people whose existence I had long ceased to be aware of begin to emerge from the fog of forgetfulness. As the mist thins, much that has remained unremembered takes shape once more and the events of over seventy years ago come into sharper relief.

I grew up and went to school in that part of south-east London bordering the Thames which embraces Woolwich, Plumstead and Shooter's Hill. Woolwich, although I did not realise it then, is a town of some historic importance, having been the home of great military and naval institutions. Its royal dockyard, established in Tudor times, was the first, and for centuries the principal, dockyard in the country. The *Great Harry* was built there in 1562 and the *Royal George* in 1751, but shipbuilding ceased in 1869 and the dockyard became a military store depot.

A little way downriver was the vast expanse of the Royal Arsenal, some 1,200 acres devoted to the sinews of war. The Arsenal developed gradually from the time of Queen Elizabeth I but it grew rapidly in the early nineteenth century, reaching its peak in terms of output and employees during the First World War. Guns, shells, torpedoes, small-arms ammunition

The main gates of the Royal Arsenal.

Powis Street, Woolwich.

and wagons were produced in huge quantities in its workshops to fuel the battles on the Western Front. The Arsenal also included experimental laboratories and extensive practice ranges on the nearby marshes. All the various engines and components of war were designed, tested and manufactured there. In the 1920s and '30s, the Arsenal and the dockyard provided much of the manual and skilled-engineering work in the town. In many families, son followed father into employment there and both places were regarded locally as rest homes for those fortunate enough to enter their gates.

I became aware early on that Woolwich was a military centre of distinction. It was the headquarters of the Royal Regiment of Artillery and the town was dominated by its great barracks, hospital, playing fields and parade ground. The RA also possessed its own garrison church, theatre, museum (the famous Rotunda) and the specialist buildings needed for men, horses and guns. Beyond this immediate area stretched the expanse of Woolwich Common, dotted with various military installations, including gun sheds, a repository, barracks and a stadium where the famous Woolwich military tattoo was held. Nearby was James Wyatt's

Royal Military Academy, cousin to that at Sandhurst. It was here, behind its long, castellated façade, complete with miniature white tower, that engineering and artillery officers were trained. It was the alma mater of Woolwich's most famous son, General George Gordon (he was born at 29 The Common in 1833), more colloquially known as 'Chinese' Gordon and later, Gordon of Khartoum.

As one might expect, many of the streets and squares in Woolwich were named after military heroes, and one heroine of the Napoleonic and Crimean Wars. Unthinkingly as a child, I walked along Nightingale Place, Wellington Street, Hill Street, Beresford Square, Raglan Road, Paget Street and Cambridge Road. Other roads had military echoes: Academy Road, Ordnance Road and Artillery Place. Indeed, a street map of Woolwich is a useful primer of military history.

I suppose Woolwich was best-known nationally for its free ferry. This was originally established in the 1880s, and when I first knew it, there were two paddle steamers, the *Will Crooks* (MP for Woolwich from 1903–21) and the *John Benn* (a former chairman of the LCC). In the 1930s these ferries carried about 20,000 passengers and 2,500 vehicles daily.

The Woolwich Free Ferry.

Shooter's Hill.

As the town spreads southwards, the ground begins to rise steadily towards Plumstead and to the imposing ridge of Shooter's Hill, over 300ft high, along which run the Old Dover Road or Watling Street. It was up Shooter's Hill that the Dover Mail lumbered in the mud on a Friday night in late November at the start of *A Tale of Two Cities*. The ridge is the southern boundary of Woolwich and Plumstead; beyond were the suburban deserts of Eltham and Well Hall. To the west, past Woolwich Common and the Royal Artillery barracks are Charlton, Blackheath and Greenwich. To the east, Woolwich merges with Plumstead and the long expanse of Plumstead Common points towards Abbey Wood and Erith.

The area was, and still is, fortunate in possessing a number of those 'lungs of London' – namely public parks and woods. Besides Woolwich and Plumstead Commons, there was Shrewsbury Park and Eaglesfield, Oxleas Woods, Jackwood, Castlewood and Crown Woods. Several of these woods and parks lie on the slopes and crest of Shooter's Hill and had been acquired by a far-sighted council to prevent development and to preserve them for the public. My favourite, Shrewsbury Park, though not quite at the top of Shooter's Hill, commanded a panorama of London

River and the City. On clear days, looking westwards beyond the shining bends of the river, you could see the dome of St Paul's eight miles away, the tallest building in the City, dominating the horizon. Immediately below lay Woolwich Reach; I remember seeing the splendid sight of the Thames sailing barges, with their brown sails and distinctive rig, plying up and down the river. To the east, the Thames wound its way out towards the estuary and the Channel, with the tall chimneys and bulk of the Ford factory at Dagenham looming in the distance.

Although we moved twice before 1939, I still grew up in an area that was only about a mile-and-a-half square. In fact, the part in which I spent most of my boyhood was even smaller, yet it managed to encompass the myriad experiences of childhood. It is strange, in retrospect, to realise how very limited it was. You never know an area so intimately as that of your childhood. Growing up slowly, moving out, on foot, from the centre, you learn an intricate network of streets and lanes and commons, much as a young policeman learns his beat. But when you move away, grow older, become a car owner, you never know your new district in this detailed way. You drive to work or to the shops along routes that hardly ever vary. You rarely walk for pleasure in towns or in the suburbs. Now, of course, children are no longer able to play in the streets or roam the district, as we once did. Within my boundaries I knew every street, lane and alley, and all their names. I had dawdled, run, chased and been pursued through them. I had walked to school, to the shops and to the parks. I knew every path and track on the commons and in the woods. I knew the names of all the shops, stalls and most of the public houses. As Ratty knew his river bank, so I knew my territory in Woolwich and Plumstead.

TWO

PARENTS &
RELATIONS

'Ere the parting hours go by
Quick, thy tablets. Memory!'

A Memory Picture, Arnold

I want to tell you something of the background of my parents and their
families so that you can understand the influence they had upon my
childhood. My father was born in 1896 in East Grinstead, a small
market town in Sussex, and lived there until 1914. His father, George, was
a carpenter and the family had been established in the town for many years.

My mother and father.

They lived at 88 Queens Road, a pleasant three-storey semi-detached house built of a soft red brick, about fifty yards from the cricket ground in nearby West Street. It was a narrow but substantial-seeming house, with a small back garden that ended treacherously in a shin-high wall and a steep drop into the cemetery. The front door, approached by a flight of stone steps, was always kept freshly whitened and rarely used. A passage sloped down the side of the house and led round to the back door, outside which stood the mighty mangle. When I first saw the living room, it contained a gas stove (the house was lit by gas) and a shallow stone sink, a kitchen range and a pantry in the corner by the back door. There was a large, pine kitchen table and dresser and the brick floor was covered with coconut matting. The rest of the ground floor consisted of a long, unlit subterranean passage leading from a corner of the living room and terminating in a lavatory raised high upon a concrete step – a throne indeed. The most fleeting of visits through there was a candle and matches job. Halfway along this passage, a curtained aperture on the right led into a low-ceilinged workshop-cum-storeroom with an earth floor, lit by a semi-basement window. Here were all kinds of objects, the bygones and discards of two generations which I enjoyed turning over. Covered in dust and hopelessly jumbled together were strange jars, sticks, boxes, tools, wire, rusty tins, wood, parts of bicycles, deck-chair frames, broken umbrellas and various kitchen utensils exhausted by years of waiting to be repaired.

On the first floor were two rooms. The rear room was a highly respectable but immensely uncomfortable sitting room, dominated by an oval painted photograph of my grandmother and a studio portrait of my father, a private in the Royal Sussex Regiment. The front room was a kind of parlour with no defined function and hardly ever used. Indeed, the back room itself only seemed to be used on Sunday afternoons for polite teas or if there were visitors. When we used to visit my father's family, we always sat and had our meals at the kitchen table downstairs but, then, we were 'family'.

My grandparents on my father's side are but shadowy figures. My grandmother died in 1932, when I was six, and I only remember a stout immobile figure in an armchair by the kitchen range. My grandfather died three years later, his thick walrus moustache, like the smile on the face of the Cheshire Cat, is the only feature about him which has endured. Considering his prowess as a cricketer, I find it surprising that he left no indelible sporting mark upon me. He was a well-known local cricketer, turning out regularly for East Grinstead, where his bowling was a great asset. He had also played for Sussex Colts but he never actually played for his county.

Myself as a baby with my parents.

While still a boy, he played in a local youth team at a time when the Australians were touring England. Each member of this team was nicknamed after an Australian cricketer and my grandfather, no doubt on grounds of alliteration and a common Christian name, was called 'Bonnor'. George Bonnor was a bearded giant of a man, 6ft 6in tall, known as 'the Australian Hercules', and a tremendous hitter. This sobriquet stuck so fast that it was subsequently attached to all male Bristows. I can remember my father being greeted in the town with 'Hey up, Bonnor' more than once. There is a pleasant story about Bonnor. Unlikely as it seems, he attended a supper at which Augustine Birrell lectured on Dr Johnson. After this daunting introduction to the works of a writer of whom he had never heard, Bonnor said, 'If I weren't Bonnor the cricketer, I should like to have been Dr Johnson.' To which Birrell replied that if Johnson had been present that night the great man would have preferred Bonnor's conversation to that of the literary critics gathered around the table.

There were seven children in the family: four boys, of whom my father (christened John Henry but always known as Jack) was the second, and three girls. All his brothers, George, the eldest, Jim and Harold, married but they produced only one son between them – Alan, George's boy.

Family group.

Of my uncles, George was a fitter employed at the Arsenal. He and his family lived on the Well Hall estate and we saw them from time to time. 'Brother Jim', as my father facetiously called him, lived in a small, un-modernised terrace house in West Street opposite the cricket ground. He drove the town's dustcart and was also a part-time fireman – but more of Jim later. Harold was the youngest of the family and I saw little of him as a child. He became a joiner and, after marrying, lived a little way out of East Grinstead at North End on the London road. So, we did not always see him when we called at Queen's Road.

My father's three sisters were quite dissimilar. Bess, the eldest of the family, kept house after her mother's death and never married. She was an ardent supporter of the Methodist chapel at the corner of West Street and a source of scarcely-suppressed merriment in a family not renowned for Sunday observance or subtle humour. Sad to say, Bess was a trifle plain with a rather heavy, mournful face. She was, however, undoubtedly a good woman. Alice married Charlie Payne, a member of the Payne tribe related to and living near the Bristows. Alice (Alley) and Charlie lived a couple of doors away in Queen's Road and we usually paid a brief call on them when visiting no. 88. After her marriage, Alley carried on working at a local solicitor's office and continued there, after Charlie died, until she retired, having completed fifty years service. Nell, the youngest, was my favourite. She was a tall, rosy-faced, well-built woman, lively and full of fun with a country woman's earthy sense of humour. I am surprised she never married because she must have had her chances, as they say, but perhaps her sense of humour got the better of her at the critical moment. She left school at fourteen and worked for over fifty years in a baby-linen shop in the town. Bristows are nothing if not long-serving! She had a quick, accurate ear for dialogue and an appreciation of the quirks and quiddities of her older relations and the eccentrics in the town. On our visits, she needed little encouragement to regale us with a string of anecdotes from her repertoire.

My mother's home was Brighton. Born in 1896, she was christened Elsie (though usually known as Else) and was the eldest of seven children, five girls and two boys. They were a close, happy and loving family and lived at 44 Totland Road, a street of small terraced houses demolished after the Second World War as part of a redevelopment scheme. Her father, Harry Potter (to whom I now realise I bear a striking resemblance) was a tailor's cutter and fated to become, in 1913, one of the first road casualties. Walking in town, he stepped off the pavement to let some women pass and was struck by one of the new motorbuses. He suffered a broken hip and died a few days later in hospital, aged forty-two, leaving a wife and seven children, six of them under fourteen. Being quite unable to provide

Roy's christening in 1928. I am standing on the left, dressed to kill.

for her family, my grandmother (known to me as 'Nana' – all grandmothers are thus known in our family) was forced to see her children split up. Her two small sons, Charles and George, were despatched to Spurgeon's Orphanage in Stockwell; three daughters, Phyllis, Gladys and Hettie, went to live with relatives in Brighton while Dorothy ('Dot'), who was rather a sickly child, stayed with her mother. My own mother, who had left school at fourteen, was already in service and away from home.

It is a tribute to Nana and to the character of her children that they overcame these disadvantages and made their way successfully in the world. Charles became a self-employed accountant and George a store manager. My mother and her sisters all went out to work and, except for Gladys ('Glad'), eventually married. Glad joined the Liverpool Police and afterwards transferred to the probation service and worked for many years in Cannock and Eastbourne. Auntie Glad was by far my favourite aunt, a tall, attractive, competent woman; it was always a mystery to us why she never married. I dimly recall whispers or half-heard rumours about a romance long ago with a naval officer that sadly came to nothing, but that was all.

Nana was one of nature's survivors. She had always been a 'bit of a lass'. At one period she and Harry had worked for a time in the evenings behind the bar of a club in Brighton. They were a pleasant, happy-go-lucky, gregarious couple with many friends. Nana, although not conventionally pretty, had bright brown eyes, a ready smile and a bubbling sense of fun. She loved a joke, enjoyed a drink, liked a game of cards (though she was a shocking loser) and took an active interest in the horses. Despite the sadness and poverty of her early married life, she was always remarkably cheerful and full of fun – I loved her very much.

I always became excited when Nana was coming to stay with us, for by this time she was my only grandparent. As soon as she came through the door, my first words to her, almost before she took her hat and coat off, were, 'Will you play cards with me, Nana?' And she unfailingly did. Together we played endless games of knockout whist, pelmanism, sevens and beggar-my-neighbour, with Ludo and snakes-and-ladders in between for a change. Throughout, Nana remained lively and amusing, and never for a moment did she give me the slightest inkling that she might have preferred to be doing something else.

My mother was a pretty young woman, 5ft 5ins in height, slim and with naturally wavy dark hair. She had an oval face, large brown eyes and neat, regular features. She was quiet, warm-hearted, capable and energetic but perhaps a little too submissive for her own good. Apart from a period during the latter part of the First World War when she worked as a

With my father and grandfather.

conductress on the Brighton buses, a miserably cold job in the bleak mid-winter, she spent her working life in service, first in Brighton but mainly in London until her marriage. You might say she remained in service after her marriage, too, because until her death she waited on my father hand and foot. This was not considered at all unusual at this time, for necessity and tradition meant that wives had to keep the breadwinner in the field. When he returned at night, exhausted by his labours, she had to be there to cherish him and cook for him, reserving the choicest morsels for his plate. This is how it had always been; daughters copied their mothers and so the pattern continued.

My mother's time in service had given her, as it gave to so many young women, a distinct refinement. She had seen life in upper-class households at first-hand and she had absorbed certain standards of speech, dress and manners. She had learned how households were organised and managed and she had acquired a wide variety of domestic skills. She tried in her quiet, modest way to introduce a little of the fruits of her experience into her own house, not always without success. Occasionally, when we were alone together, she would talk about her time in service, prefacing her remarks with, 'I remember once when I was with Lord Joycey . . .' Sometimes she would come out with sayings she had picked up, such as, 'You can always tell a lady by her feet and a gentleman by his neck.' Her background sometimes led to differences with my father, who had not been exposed to her advantages, but he was sensible enough to realise his good fortune in securing such an attractive, competent wife. Theirs was a useful partnership, as he worked hard to secure his place on the lower-middle-class rungs of the ladder of life.

My father was a slim, dark-haired man, the same height as my mother, with an open, pleasant face and a ready smile. I think it is fair to say that my father was regarded by his own family as the one who had 'got on' – a view he shared with them. He was not a skilled craftsman like George or Harold, or a member of the dustcart team like Jim, but a white-collar worker. He was a clerk, a dark-suited employee, paid monthly, who started at 9 a.m., worked sitting down, and enjoyed a non-contributory pension. He was a man who wrote a fair hand and kept records, interviewed the undeserving poor, made calculations and handled money. He had not only served abroad during the First World War but he had left East Grinstead and moved to London. Invested with the aura of the big city, he tended to patronise his relations in East Grinstead and referred to them quite shamelessly as country bumpkins.

Because of the nature of his work, he established himself early on as something of an authority upon the life and habits of the London poor. If he stressed their shortcomings, I suspect it was partly to point out what a smart and able chap Jack was. This was acceptable within his family but slight tensions sometimes arose when he met my mother's relatives. Although they had had an unfortunate start to their lives, they were of a much more formidable mettle than my father's family. Even at the modest level at which they lived and worked, they were unwilling to be patronised. They considered my mother to have done quite well for herself, though my father's *amour propre* would have been wounded if he had known that he was regarded by her family as a bit of a country bumpkin himself. Certainly, when in his mid-twenties, my father was a lively fellow, a young man with a fund of jokes and tales, mainly derived from his army service. Jack, in fact, was rather a lad and my gentle mother always referred to his being 'the life and soul of the party'.

My father was a slow but steady and reliable worker (a pace bequeathed to all his four sons by their father), and his domestic life revolved round his home, his wife and son. He rarely had a drink and was never a man for pubs and clubs or for the dogs and horses. He was mildly interested in football and cricket and he occasionally turned out for his office cricket side. He was a kind and affectionate father, genuinely fond of children, and he always had plenty of time to spare for me.

Theirs was a successful marriage. I was never conscious as a child of any tensions between them and I certainly cannot remember any 'words' or rows. We were, simply, that not unusual institution – an ordinary, happy family.

THREE

AUNTIE WALTERS

'Come to me, come to me! When the cruel shame and terror
you have so long fled from, most beset you, come to me! I am
the relieving officer appointed by eternal ordinance to do my
work; I am not held in estimation according as I shirk it.'

Our Mutual Friend, Charles Dickens

My father met my mother at a party in Brighton on Christmas
Eve, 1914, while he was on leave from the army. They wrote to
each other during his time at Gallipoli, in Egypt and Palestine,
although his side of the correspondence was necessarily limited to picture
postcards and the standard buff-coloured military postcard of the 'I am
well/not well' and 'I have been admitted into hospital: sick/wounded'
variety. In 1919 he returned to England, coming first by sea from
Alexandria to Taranto and then by an interminable rail journey in wooden
carriages across Europe to Boulogne. Their relationship flourished; they
became engaged and in March 1923 they were married at St Peter's
Church, Brighton.

During the immediate post-war years, my father worked in East
Grinstead while my mother worked for one or two families in London as a
cook or cook/housekeeper and lived in. After their marriage, he moved up
to Woolwich and they lodged with an elderly widow called Mrs Walters at
67 Durham Road, on a curving hill that leads up towards Plumstead
Common. Towards the end of 1925, with my mother pregnant, they
moved into a rented terraced house in Tuam Road, close to the common.

Plumstead Common was surrounded by streets of terraced villas built
around the turn of the century. Speculative they may have been, but they
were tolerably well constructed for the period of stock London brick with
an eye, enthusiastic rather than exact, for architectural detail. They had
bay windows on the ground floor and some even sported bays on the first
floor. The windows had stone lintels and the bays were supported by
columns of no known order. Some were plain and some were fluted, but

most had foliated capitals giving a faintly Doric or Corinthian flavour to the façade. Much care was paid to the front porches. These had pointed stone arches or, as in our case, a semi-circular arch with a decorated keystone. Inside the porch, the sides were often tiled to shoulder height and occasionally there was an attractive fanlight over the door. 111 Tuam Road was typical of these houses and was further embellished by a projecting slated hip over the first-floor bay.

Here at no. 111, I was born on 31 March 1926, a hot Easter Monday. Had my mother's labour been even further prolonged, I should have arrived on April Fool's Day, which would have caused me much embarrassment. I discovered later that being born towards the end of the financial year has certain administrative advantages. I was christened Adrian John. My first name was a most unusual one in those days; the only other Adrian people had heard of was Sir Adrian Boult, with whom I became amusingly associated for years. When I asked my mother why they had called me Adrian, she told me that in one of the upper-class establishments in which she had worked there was a family friend with this name. She found his name, Adrian Honey, so delightful and euphonious that she determined to bestow it upon any son she might produce.

'Burden with' rather than 'bestow' would have been more appropriate. For several years, when asked by well-meaning grown-ups what my name was, I was unable to get my childish tongue round Adrian. The best I could do, after much effort and grimacing, was 'Agey'. This distortion was taken up by my parents and stuck fast, so Agey I became. But worse was to follow. In the manner of Christian names, 'Agey' was found to be too cumbersome and was abbreviated to 'Age'. I was called this at home for many years. I was even referred to sometimes as 'Old Age' in much the same way as friends might say, 'What's old Jack doing up in the shed?' It was a grotesque name for a small boy. Strangers around me were mystified when they heard the cry, 'Age!' or 'Where's Old Age?' and even more puzzled when I responded. As a postscript I might add that in adolescence I suffered agonies of embarrassment over my wretched name. I felt there were already enough embarrassments at this time, both physical and social, without having to bear this particular one. At one point, I even decided to call myself by another name and did so for a time. It all seems rather silly now.

I have no memory of no. 111, although I spent my first three years there. I have some snaps of this period revealing me as a toddler with a mass of curls in a pinafore-type dress. There are also shots of a solemn, chubby child on the common who has graduated to a knitted suit and is carrying his first cricket bat. Holiday pictures of Brighton, Bognor and

Southsea show me building sandcastles or sprawling on the wet sand. No doubt I was taken down to the Bristows at East Grinstead and to the Potters at Brighton to be passed round and generally admired but, regrettably, I can remember nothing of it.

In the same month as I was born, my father was appointed, through the influence of a distant uncle (Uncle Mark), assistant relieving officer to the West Woolwich District of the Woolwich Union under the Board of Guardians (i.e. Guardians of the Poor), at a salary of £205 per annum. The Board of Guardians stemmed from the Poor Law Act of 1834 and was responsible for administering the system of Poor Law relief. In 1930, their responsibilities were transferred to the London County Council, re-organised and divided into two main areas – the care of the sick and the administration of the Poor Law. Eventually, this work was unified in the National Assistance Board. At the time of my father's appointment, his work consisted mainly of granting assistance to the many unemployed in the area who could not manage on their unemployment benefit. This was primarily because of the rise in the cost of living after the war and the static nature of the scale of relief. The demand for public assistance was increased by the effects of the General Strike of 1926.

I mention this in some detail because my father was to stay in this field, next under the LCC and then under the National Assistance Board, until he retired at the age of sixty-five. This meant that he was in secure pensionable employment all his life. If his salary was modest, he was never exposed to the threat of unemployment and was able to take on the purchase of a small house with a quiet mind. This good fortune was unexceptionable, being shared with hundreds and thousands of others. Yet for a man who spent most of his adult working life relieving the necessitous, giving assistance to the sick, the old, the unemployed, the homeless and to tramps, he displayed surprisingly little sympathy with their varied and lamentable situations. He used to condemn the unemployed as feckless, work-shy scroungers and his only objective with the tramps and other itinerants was to move them on as quickly as possible at minimum expense. He dispensed assistance grudgingly, as though the tiny sums involved were liable to be deducted from his monthly salary. He must have been an exemplary officer.

Even though he had married and left Mrs Walters, my father still remained in touch with her, and from my earliest days I was taken round to see her. I always called her 'Auntie Walters'. This is not as curious as it may sound. I already had a large collection of legitimate relatives to which I added, like most children I knew, several surrogate aunts and uncles who were friends of my parents. They simply became known as 'Auntie Doris' or 'Uncle Bill'. It seemed quite natural and they were happy to be thus

Mother, Auntie Walters and I.

called. There were also a few older acquaintances of my parents who, either because of age or tenuous relationship, were always known to me by their surnames prefixed by 'Auntie' or 'Uncle', thus Auntie Smith and Uncle Barber.

Auntie Walters was one of the latter. She lived in a neat terraced house with a front door that had coloured glass panels in it. Once inside, you were led down a narrow, gas-lit passage, the tiled floor covered with oilcloth, and into the front room. This gloomy room, I now realise, was furnished to the late-Victorian taste, dating from the early days of her marriage. Mr Walters, a shadowy figure, who had apparently worked at the Arsenal, was never mentioned. When we called, Auntie Walters sat in a large, spoon-backed upholstered chair by a roaring coal fire. She invariably wore an ankle-length black dress, black shoes and stockings. The bodice of her dress was ruched and pleated and ornamented with beads of jet, which gleamed in the firelight. She had a lined, leathery face, from which sprouted whiskers. I did not enjoy kissing her.

Auntie Walters used to tend the fire with vigour. She poked it, raked it, heaped coals upon it and enlivened it with the fire irons that rested on the edge of the brass tender. Sometimes I sat on a stool at her feet in front of the fire and watched the pictures in the glowing coals, drowsily unaware of the talk above me.

Usually, I sat or lay against a cushion on a red plush sofa which occupied one wall. Over this was fixed a large glass case containing stuffed songbirds arranged on artificial branches forming a tableau labelled 'Who killed Cock Robin?' Robin himself, with a tiny arrow stuck in his blood-stained chest, hung dejectedly from a lower branch. Two more glass cases were secured to the opposite wall over the sideboard. One held a stuffed barn owl, with a fierce and menacing look in his shiny glass eyes. In the other was a creature I found fascinating but repellent. It was a stuffed kitten, a sorry-looking creature, which in addition to the usual four legs, one at each corner, had a fifth leg sticking up at right angles from the middle of its back.

We usually called about teatime on a Saturday or Sunday afternoon. We had a light tea and then, after a decent interval, Auntie Walters would produce a bottle of homemade wine and a tin box of wine-biscuits from her sideboard. I think she made the wine herself, although I never saw any signs of manufacture in her dark little kitchen. I have never since come across such biscuits; we certainly never had them at home. They were plump, puffy, cream-coloured objects, made in various shapes, not sweet, but soft to the tooth with a consistency not unlike a commercially grown mushroom. Even as a tiny boy I was always given a glass of wine plus a couple of these unusual biscuits. The heat of the fire and the

Who's a pretty boy, then?

stuffiness of the room, plus the strength of Auntie's homemade wine, soon made me drowsy and I keeled slowly over against my mother and fell asleep.

We had moved in 1929 to a larger terraced house in Herbert Road, which I suppose was about a mile and a half from Durham Road, and it is here that memory-proper begins for me. I remember that when it was time to leave Auntie Walters, my father used to hoist me onto his shoulders where I fastened my little gaitered legs round his neck and clung on to his head for dear life. Home we trudged, through the gas-lit streets where, half-asleep, I was gently unloaded on to my bed, undressed and slipped quickly between the sheets. As I grew older, I was not quite so overcome by the wine and I was able to walk back to Herbert Road through the dark streets holding my father's hand. I remember the peculiar warmth of his hand on cold nights and I can feel the sensation, even now, of his warm dry palm as I slipped my hand into his.

When we called upon Auntie Walters in spring or summer, at some stage during our visit the four of us would go outside to scrutinise her garden. This was a small pocket-handkerchief of earth bisected by a concrete path with black wavy ceramic edging that ended abruptly at a fence made of sleepers at the top of a steep railway embankment. My father was regarded by Auntie Walters as something of a gardener. Whether this was because he came from the country or because he grew a few vegetables of his own, I am not sure. Perhaps it was simply because he was a man and therefore assumed to be knowledgeable about such things. Auntie Walters deferred to his views and recommendations. He leaned against the water butt where she drowned unwanted kittens (unless they had more than the usual quota of legs) and dispensed advice, while my mother surreptitiously plucked small weeds from the flowerbeds.

This inspection of back gardens was a ritual in our family circle. On any visit to relatives or friends, we used to go out to the back, stand in a knowing line on the concrete paths and solemnly inspect the short, tight rows of vegetables. These were normally lettuce, beetroot, radishes, onions and carrots grown from packets of 'Bees Seeds that Grow' bought at Woolworths. We admired the cabbages and Brussels sprouts, the screen of runner beans, and paid tribute to the herbaceous border full of traditional cottage-garden flowers – stocks, gladioli, Canterbury bells, daisies, wallflowers, lupins and chrysanthemums. We commiserated over greenfly and black fly, nodding knowingly over slugs, cats and snails and deplored the lack of rain. After all, I suppose most of the aunties and uncles we visited in London were only one generation away from villages and small country towns. For them, a 'nice' garden, apart from its obvious links and benefits, indicated an attitude to property and social responsibility.

In my car with Auntie Hett.

As I grew older, our visits to Durham Road became less frequent. I still used to call on the old lady from time to time until the outbreak of war because a close friend of mine, Ralph Bugg, lived opposite her. We lost touch with her finally in 1941, when my father was transferred to Tunbridge Wells, and it was not until some years later that we learned that Auntie Walters had died peacefully in the last summer of the war.

FOUR

EARLY DAYS &
ARMY WAYS

'And I'm learnin' 'ere in London
wot the ten-year soldier tells:
If you'd 'eard the East a-callin',
you won't never 'eed naught else.'

Mandalay, Kipling

Our new house in Herbert Road was close to a short row of shops dominated by a branch of the Royal Arsenal Co-operative Society and opposite the Methodist church. No. 164 was a two-storey terraced villa with a basement and a modest garden at the back. In the front was a low brick wall, behind which the ground sloped steeply to the area in front of the basement window, or 'airey' as we always called it. Thus you approached the front door across what was almost a little bridge from the pavement. It was not until many years later (I am embarrassed to say how many) that I realised that our road had been named after Sidney Herbert, the Secretary for War during the Crimean War, and the supporter and friend of Florence Nightingale.

I soon found out that around the corner in Paget Rise, lived another branch of the Bristow family. They were only distantly related but they became closer to us in the next decade than most of our close relations. Arthur and Elsie Bristow had one daughter, Marjorie, and three sons, Eric, Leslie and Peter. Peter, the youngest, was a couple of years older than me but I came to look upon him as an older and loftier brother. As I grew up, I may well have worshipped him a little. . . .

Living with them was the formidable Uncle Mark, Arthur's father, who had been instrumental in getting my father a post with the Board of Guardians. Uncle Mark was well over 6ft tall, broad-shouldered and, with his closely cropped head and walrus moustache, an imposing figure. He had been in the Metropolitan Police and was station sergeant at Woolwich until he retired to become a relieving officer. No potential offender welcomed a blow from his rolled-up cape and he had little trouble with drunks, wife-beaters and other excitables.

My recollections of the three years spent in Herbert Road are dominated by school and by the army. But first I must grow up a little. One event marking a milestone in my childhood was my being 'breeched' (my mother's term) when I was three and a bit. When I started walking,

Breeched that morning!

I wore a pinafore dress and later a smock or short coat over I am not sure what, and a knitted suit in colder weather. Now the time had come for me to go into my first pair of proper short trousers. I can remember standing outside the front door in my new corduroy shorts, squinting into the sun while I had my photograph taken. Suddenly, I became recognisable as a small boy with a good head of wavy brown hair. Gone was the mass of auburn curls of which my mother was inordinately proud. She delighted in telling how people used to stop her when she was out wheeling me in my pram to admire her child's striking crop. It may well have happened once, but I found out many years later that my mother tended to inflate a single occurrence into a recurring pattern. For example, if we were talking about a certain café, she would say, 'Oh, yes, we always used to go there for our dinner' – she had been once. Or, if we mentioned a music-hall star she would comment, 'We used to see him a lot in the old days.' I suspect she had probably seen him only once, but it was a harmless foible.

I first became aware of the army when we went for walks on Woolwich Common or caught a tram down into Beresford Square. Beyond our house and the shops, Herbert Road curved round to the right, merging into Academy Road and opening out a splendid view of the Royal Military Academy, which appeared like some toy fort across a great polo field.

The Royal Military Academy.

The Royal Artillery Barracks.

Academy Road continued with the common on the left and then, suddenly, there was the immense expanse of the parade ground and the barracks of the Royal Artillery stretching into the distance. Facing the end of the parade-ground stood St George's Church, the religious focus for the garrison which at this time numbered between 4,500 and 5,000 men. The Royal Artillery band used to perform concerts in this handsome church. The names of those of the regiment who had won the Victoria Cross were recorded on the walls of the apse.

The building that gripped my imagination most was the Rotunda. This exotic fantasy was based on one of the double-ceiling tents Nash had designed for the meeting of allied sovereigns at Carlton House Gardens in 1814. Donated by the Prince Regent, it was made into a permanent structure by Nash in 1820, with the addition of a leaden roof and a central pillar to carry the extra weight. This superb twenty-four-sided regular polygon resembled nothing more than a vast Indian tent and was the home of the Museum of Artillery and its fascinating contents.

The common was separated from the parade ground and the barracks by the Ha-Ha Road; a curious name which puzzled me for years until I learned it meant a sunken road surrounding a mansion to prevent deer or

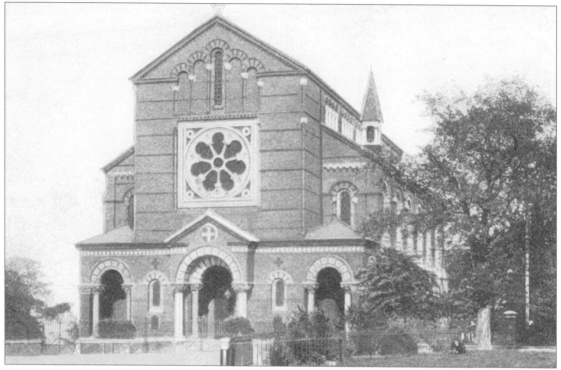

St George's Church.

cattle from straying onto the lawns and gardens. At the intersections of the roads and paths which criss-crossed the common were a tank and various howitzers and field guns from the First World War.

I suppose the common is identified in my mind with the Woolwich military tattoo, which was reckoned to be second only to the one at Aldershot and was held in the stadium. A visit to the tattoo, like going, when I was a little older, to the Royal Artillery Theatre and to the pantomime at the Lyceum, was one of the highlights of my year. The music, colour and action, the rattle and thunder of the horse-drawn guns and limbers as the teams raced around the stadium, the crack of the blank rounds and the smoke of battle I found profoundly exciting. All this was heightened as darkness fell and the arena was lit with searchlights. All the traditional elements in the Woolwich tattoo culminated in a grand finale, which was often the staging of some particular assault or incident in an eighteenth- or nineteenth-century battle. The main gate of the stadium was built up to represent a fort or battlements, and I still remember vividly one year when a body of redcoats advanced under fire and stormed a floodlit fort amid a fusillade of musket fire and clouds of coloured smoke.

Woolwich was full of military activity. I saw squads of soldiers drilling on the parade ground, groups being doubled off for PE and men being marched off to installations on the common. Convalescent patients, in their ill-fitting hospital blues, white shirts and red ties, drifted around the hospital and down to the dispensary. Officers, immaculate in riding breeches, highly polished boots and Sam Browns, were occasionally glimpsed too.

On fine Sunday mornings, my father often took me down to the barracks to see the church parade. This was a free spectacle and a popular diversion for the neighbourhood. We set off to arrive at the parade ground a little while before the service in the garrison church ended and positioned ourselves opposite the central arch, the entrance to the barracks, and close to the saluting base. After the service, the troops filed out and formed up to a buzz of anticipation in the crowd. The senior officer, frequently the General, moved up to the saluting base with his aides. There were distant, high-pitched words of command, then the thrilling thunder of the drums and the Royal Artillery band struck up the regimental march, 'The British Grenadiers'. With the sergeant-major, resplendent at its head, twirling his mace in his white-gloved hand, the band marched down the parade ground, leading the long columns of men towards the saluting base. Officers with drawn swords led their companies or units and gave an 'eyes right!' as they approached the dais. When they reached the end of the parade ground, the columns wheeled to the right and disappeared into the rear of the barracks. By the time the last units were passing the saluting base, the band had made its way back through the central arch. Then, right in front of us, it played a series of stirring marches, marching and counter-marching with a precision that was quietly but deeply admired. The parade ended with a short concert. The band formed a circle, band boys brought out music stands and scores, and the bandmaster conducted a selection of popular favourites, including the local one, 'Wait for the Wagon'. Slowly the crowd dispersed and we walked home looking forward to our Sunday roast dinner.

The Royal Artillery band was popular and highly regarded in the district. As well as its ceremonial and mess functions, it played regularly at the Valley (Charlton Athletic's football ground), gave concerts of popular classics in the garrison church and appeared at a variety of civic, charitable and sporting occasions. My mother, Auntie Elsie and her brother Stan used to attend the concerts at St George's and, on one or two occasions, took me with them. This was my introduction to serious music.

This musical interest was stimulated further by that most keenly anticipated of treats, a visit to the Royal Artillery Theatre which stood near the garrison church and just around the corner from the end of the

A church parade with the Royal Artillery Band.

barracks. These visits were my first experience of the theatre and gave me an enthusiasm and love for the stage from which I have never recovered. I do not know if the productions I saw there were professional touring shows or amateur operatic societies but, like all children, I was spellbound. I sat on my father's folded overcoat in the pit stalls and gazed at the profusion of gilt and red plush around me. Slowly, the boxes and the stalls filled up and I watched the orchestra come in and start tuning up. Then came the magical moment when the lights were dimmed, the house was hushed and the great red curtains parted to reveal a world of enchantment. Spectacle, colour, music! I sat transfixed by the brilliance of it all. I was especially thrilled by 'The Student Prince' and its resounding chorus ending with, 'And to hell with Burgundy!' At Christmas came the best treat of all, the visit to the pantomime on Boxing Day. I enjoyed this even more than the musicals because of the dames and the comedy scenes.

My father, incidentally, had decided views on the worth of any theatrical production he attended. In his eyes, plays with a small number of characters had little merit. He judged productions purely on the size of the cast, so any musical comedy had a head start. However, if the entertainment included animals, his rule of thumb was that any animal was worth two actors. So the production of *Chu Chin Chow* he saw as a young man was always top of his list. He was a great one for spectacle.

If my first musical and theatrical experiences are derived from the Royal Artillery Theatre, many of my early memories are suffused by talk of the army and the First World War. Sadly, its legacies were not far to seek, not only in an army town like Woolwich, but in almost every town and village. I was conscious even then of the number of men you saw in the town who had been blinded in the war, men with only one leg, or no legs, the prevalence of crutches and of men with empty sleeves pinned across their jackets. Doctors had found it difficult to identify and control the infection caused by the dirt and filth of the trenches in serious wounds, and amputation was often the only means of preventing the spread of gas gangrene. In Beresford Square and Powis Street, I often saw small groups of ex-servicemen, some wearing their medals pinned to their jackets or shabby overcoats, playing popular tunes of the day or the old songs of the trenches on various musical instruments as they drifted along the gutter.

Domestic influences were powerful and insistent. At the outbreak of war, of the East Grinstead Bristows, George, the eldest son, being an engineering craftsman working at the Arsenal, was in a reserved occupation and remained there for the duration. My father had already joined the Territorials in 1913, like many of the young men in the town, and in August 1914 he was mustered into the 4th Battalion of the Royal Sussex Regiment. Virtually all his friends found themselves in France early the following year with the 2nd and 5th Battalions. The 2nd Battalion took part in the disastrous attack on Aubers Ridge near Neuve Chapelle on 9 May 1915 and suffered grievous losses. Few of my father's friends survived the battle; none survived the war on the Western Front.

Meanwhile, my father landed with the 4th Battalion at Sulva Bay in Gallipoli in August 1915. Like thousands of others, he was struck down with dysentery and was evacuated to Malta by hospital ship where he spent some months convalescing. Later, he rejoined the battalion in Egypt and was attached to the 160th Brigade Light Trench Mortar Battery. The 53rd Division, now part of Allenby's Army, advanced against the Turks from El Arish (First and Second Battles of Gaza) to Beersheba and on to Jerusalem and Jericho. After Allenby's victory, the 1/4th Royal Sussex entrained for France in June 1918. Fortunately, my father was not among them; he was transferred to the 1/7th Royal Welsh Fusiliers, who needed men with his training and experience. Thus he missed the last offensives on the Western Front and, after four years in the Middle East, he returned home in 1919 – still a private and without a scratch.

His younger brother, Jim, volunteered when he became of age and eventually found himself in the 12th Battalion of the Rifle Brigade in the Ypres Salient on the Western Front. Here he received a nasty dose of gas in 1918 and was invalided out with a small pension. The gas left him with a fearful, racking cough which doubled him up and left him crimson in the face, choking and gasping for breath.

Elsie's husband, Arthur, did not serve in the war (I believe he was medically unfit) but was a man obsessed by the army and by the Royal Artillery in particular. He could reel off the various batteries and brigades which had been stationed at Woolwich over many years, plus the names of their commanding officers. He died in early middle age and I did not know him for long. It was different, however, with Elsie's brother, Stan, who was my father's age and had spent the war in France as a trooper in the Royal Horse Artillery. In his later years, and I saw him only on rare occasions, I tried to draw him out about his experiences on the Western Front. Like a number of his contemporaries he did not want to talk about what he had seen and done. All I could get from him was that he was permanently hungry and that, on one occasion at least, he found himself firing over open sights into advancing German infantry.

But when he, Arthur, and my father got together, or when my father and Jim met on our visits to East Grinstead, the air was thick with reminiscence. I sat in a corner and pretended to read as the old stories of adventures behind the line and on leave were repeated. Foreign countries and their curious inhabitants were paraded and dismissed, while bewildering slang embroidered tall tales of army days and army ways. I went, reluctantly, up to bed. My father also talked freely to me at home about his experiences in Gallipoli and Malta, and of what he had seen and the places he had visited in the Middle East. So I grew up in a welter of confused pictures of army life in which bully-beef, barbed wire, condensed milk, Gurkhas, trench-mortars, plum and apple, Australians, estaminets, Jerusalem and Turks were inextricably mixed. These impressions were underlined by my father's old postcard album and by his photograph album with its snaps, yellowing and indistinct today, of him and his friends in the desert.

These strands of my childhood combined over the years to give me a lasting interest in military history and a fascination with the war on the Western Front. The scale of the carnage and the courage and endurance of the troops in conditions of unbelievable desolation haunted my imagination and filled me, like so many others, with a variety of emotions that do not dim with time.

FIVE

A MIXED INFANT

'Babies do not want to hear about babies: they like to be
told of giants and castles, and of somewhat which can
stretch and stimulate their little minds.'

Dr Johnson

It was while we lived in Herbert Road that I acquired my toy box. It
was a large wooden box, stained black without a lid and lined with
floral-patterned wallpaper. It was quite large enough for me to climb
into and it became by turns a boat, a cave or a house, according to which
story or character was exercising my imagination at the time. I could also
scramble on top of it and transform it into a hill, a castle or a rock. It was
an all-purpose box and into it went my toys, jigsaws, bricks and the
transient possessions of childhood.

It is the wooden bricks I remember best. They were not proper building
bricks with pillars and arches like the box I was given later, but educational
and decorative ones which I used for building unsteady structures. I had
three sets. One was a set of twenty-six small alphabet bricks with pictures
of animals glued onto them, ranging from A for Antelope to Z for Zebra.
Another set consisted of sixteen large cubes. Each cube had part of a
picture on every face so that when laid flat in the correct order the bricks
formed a complete picture. Thus, by reversing, turning and revolving the
cubes, six separate pictures could be formed. The pictures were sepia-
coloured and not very attractive; elves, fairies and goblins predominated
rather in the manner of poor mad Richard Dadd. My rectangular bricks
were the most interesting. They were about an inch thick, and along one
edge was a picture of a soldier in red tunic and busby so that when the
bricks were stood on end they formed a line of soldiers. When the bricks
were laid flat, they illustrated the career of Jumbo, the famous Victorian
circus elephant, and his sad and spectacular death. A couple of years later,
when I had ceased to play with them, all my bricks were given away to a
small child 'from a poor home', as my mother delicately put it.

Myself with the family pet.

Like most of us, I am intrigued and moved by the contents of the museums of childhood. There are few objects which bring the past more vividly and more movingly to life than the toys we once played with. My toy box stayed with me throughout my childhood and beyond, eventually being stood on end and acquiring shelves and a curtain as my tastes developed. I lost track of it in the war but found it again in 1984, when my father went into a rest home and we had to clear his basement flat. In one corner of the coal cellar, unregarded, riddled with woodworm and with the wallpaper peeling from the inside, stood my old toy box. My father had stored old paint tins and flowerpots in it. Sadly, it was too far gone to be passed on to my grandson and I took it with a heavy heart to the local tip.

There were two incidents involving my mother which etched themselves in my memory at this time. On Saturdays, she did much of her weekend shopping in Beresford Square market. One winter afternoon she had been out shopping as usual and at teatime we heard someone knocking at the front door. It was my mother in tears. My father led her into the sitting room. Her basket was empty. She sat on the sofa sobbing her heart out, her shoulders shaking, while my father tried to comfort her. I sat nonplussed opposite. I had never seen anything like this before. In between her tears she told us that when she went to pay for some meat, she found that someone had stolen her purse with all her housekeeping money in it. My father reported the loss to the police station but nothing ever came of it. I do not think I ever saw my mother cry so bitterly and for so long ever again – even though I am ashamed to admit that my father and I almost reduced this kind and gentle soul to tears on several occasions in later life.

The other incident does me no credit at all. Even when we are much older we are still ashamed to remember things we said and did as children. Memory is punishing and relentless on occasions and when so much has faded or disappeared from our recollection, embarrassing scenes and conversations we thought buried forever surface to wound us. Just so with the affair of the Indian war bonnet.

Like most boys, I was fascinated by Indians. For my birthday I had been given an Indian suit consisting of a fringed jerkin with mock-Indian designs painted on it and a pair of fringed trousers, but it had no feathered headdress. I was unwilling to settle for a headband with a feather stuck in the back. Nothing would satisfy me but a chief's headdress with feathers stuck in round the headband and sidepieces cascading round my shoulders. My mother set to. She made the basic headband and sides and then laboriously sewed on the feathers she had collected from the garden and the local park. At last it was finished. I changed into my Indian suit, took my new war bonnet, went into the garden, put it on and gazed at my reflection in the kitchen window. I was furious. The feathers in the headdress, instead of sticking up straight like those of the Indian warriors in my books, hung limply across my forehead at all angles. I stormed back into the kitchen where my mother was busy at the sink, flung the headdress on the floor, crying out, 'That's no good. I can't wear a thing like that!'

Other mothers would have knocked me across the kitchen but my mother simply looked hurt. She quickly took up the headdress and tried to get the feathers to stand up straight but it was impossible. We tacitly agreed to abandon the idea because by this time I realised in a dim childish way that I had deeply upset her. It was never referred to again. I had the grace to feel ashamed. The next day I became a cowboy instead, using a girl's velour school hat my mother obtained from a friend as a sombrero – black, as befitted a young baddie.

In September 1931, when I was five-and-a-half-years-old, it was time for me to start school. My mother took me up the hill to become a mixed infant at Plum Lane Infant School in Nithdale Road under the benevolent despotism of Miss Brownlee. The school had been built in 1903 by the London School Board on the steep hill below Shrewsbury Park at the junction of Nithdale Road and Plum Lane, a reminder of the days when this part of Kent was full of orchards and market gardens. Directly below the infant school, with a horrifying drop to its playground, lay Plum Lane Senior School. Our top playground was edged with a tall stout wire-mesh fence to stop innocent infants toppling over and crashing on to the asphalt below. The senior school was not the school for 'big boys' as such – to us, 'big boys' were those seven- to eleven-year-olds in the junior school, my next leap forward. No, this school was for boys aged eleven to fourteen, who had not passed the scholarship exam and had even failed to qualify for the Central School. They appeared young men of unbelievable dimensions, fearsome aspect and unvarying pugnacity. Luckily, we had virtually no contact with them since, because the schools were built into the side of a hill, our entrances were in different roads. It was conveyed to us early on, subtly but unmistakably, that these boys were rather rough, not very clever and to be avoided at all costs.

I liked Plum Lane. I remember that my mother had to make a small mat for me to kneel on in the hall at morning prayers after the registers had been marked. I could already read; like all the other children in my class I had been taught to read at home and I took to school life like a duck to water. There were no tears or problems and I soon made several bosom friends. Together we played games of Cowboys and Indians during playtime, racing about the playground smacking our backsides and urging our horses on to even greater efforts. Imaginary arrows smacked into small, heaving chests, bullets cracked viciously from our tiny fists, extravagant death throes marked the end of the war party and triumphant cowboys rode slowly back into their sunlit classrooms. At first my mother took me to school every morning, but very soon she was able to leave me without a backward look and I made my own way home. Only one incident stained my enjoyable and uneventful first year.

I often came home with my new friend, Georgie Gibson. One afternoon we came across a horse-drawn milk-cart belonging to Express Dairies standing in the road with the milkman nowhere in sight. Georgie dared me to pull the horse's tail. I ducked under the shafts, clutched a handful of hairs, gave a sharp, downward tug and ducked out again in one sinuous movement. The docile horse, surprised, lurched a few yards forward, stopped and looked round mournfully. But we had fled. Unfortunately, I had been seen by a neighbour who was able to identify me. She was round like a shot the next morning to see Miss Brownlee and soon afterwards I was called to her room. There she faced me with my crime, giving chapter and verse. I had to admit to it all. She gave me a good talking to, dwelling at some length on the damage that horses pulling milk-carts might do if they were made to bolt by the stupid actions of mindless little boys. She rummaged around in a corner and produced a cane. I had never seen one before and I did not know she possessed one. All I knew about canes was the good-humoured warnings from relatives when I started school that I had better look out or I would get the stick. A stick was never used at home – my father or mother would normally box my ears if I had been naughty. My legs trembled and I was close to tears. Miss Brownlee told me to take the cane and stand in the corner of her room. I did so with some relief but still unsure whether I was going to get it or not – much as Miss Brownlee intended no doubt. I continued standing there, confused and apprehensive, until the bell went for playtime. The headmistress then dismissed me with a further caution and I slunk away wondering why Georgie had got away scot-free.

About this time we moved to a new home at 88 Frederick Place, off Burrage Road. My parents had been saving hard for a deposit to put down on a house of their own and they had now found one they liked and could afford. It was not in such a desirable area as Herbert Road, with its military ambience. The new house was one of a street of terraced houses halfway down the hill to Woolwich. Nevertheless, it was ours (or would be in twenty years) and my father had joined the ranks of owner-occupiers. Living in Frederick Place meant a longer walk to school, but after several dummy runs with my mother, I used to go to and fro on my own, even though it meant crossing Plumstead Common Road, a busy main road even then.

At the beginning of my second year, I went up into the top class to work under the sharp-featured, caustic senior teacher, Miss Baynes. There was no nonsense in her class. She was a splendid teacher and we made rapid progress. I sat next to a plump, motherly girl called Ethel who had black hair cut in an Eton crop. I shall always be grateful to Ethel because she taught me how to tie bows on my shoes. I have a photograph of us taken on Empire Day, 1933, in the playground. At that time, Empire Day was an important occasion in the school summer calendar, surpassed solely by Armistice Day in November. We dressed up in costumes representing the dominions and colonies and paraded up and down the playground with

Empire Day at Plum Lane School.

their flags. Special prayers were offered up for those in lands beyond the seas. In this picture I am, inevitably, wearing my Indian suit (a trifle short in the leg by this time) while Ethel stands foursquare in white in the centre as Britannia, complete with trident, shield and a gold cardboard helmet. She looks every inch a future WI president.

It often happens at school that small boys team up with large boys. There is nothing improper in this (I am speaking of day schools); there is a sense of giving and receiving protection plus the attraction of opposites, the quick and lively finding its complement in the slow and stately. Reggie Walker was a very large boy indeed and eventually we became friendly and started to go home together. That summer there was a craze for playing 'horses'. Two boys would link arms behind their backs and career round the playground. Reggie and I started doing this with Reggie shouting his personal war cry of 'jolly old shit-bum' at the top of his voice. I do not know where he first heard it or whether he made it up but I never heard anyone else use it, then or since.

We tried this once too often on the way home. We were not exactly a matched pair as horses go. Off we galloped down Nithdale Road, bursting through the waiting mothers, with Reggie yelling 'jolly old shit-bum!' Suddenly, our feet became entangled and, with our arms locked behind our backs, we pitched violently forward. My head hit the pavement and everything went black, the darkness lit only by a few stars. It took me a few seconds to come round. Dazed, I put my hand up to my forehead and found blood on my fingers. Reggie, luckily, was unscathed. He propped me up against the low garden wall of a house, gave me his none-too-clean handkerchief and ran off to fetch my mother. They were soon back, breathless and anxious. My mother bandaged my head and carried me home (no mean feat), as I was too groggy to walk. She put me straight to bed and was relieved the next morning to find that nothing was cracked or broken. I carry the scar on my temple still. And Reggie and I never attempted to play 'horses' again.

I was now seven years old. I had laboured creditably under Miss Baynes at my three Rs and that summer I said goodbye to her and Ethel forever. No more mixed infants or mixed anything for me in future. I was bound for a new masculine world of education where the sexes were strictly segregated. At a stroke I was to be transformed into a junior boy. In August, my mother bought me my new cap and tie from the school outfitters in Powis Street and I prepared to meet the challenge of Fox Hill Junior School and its well-known head, Cyril Bull.

SIX

HOUSE & GARDEN

'The chief advantage of London is that a man is
always so near his burrow.'

Dr Johnson

Before we set foot in Fox Hill and meet Cyril Bull, I must tell you
something about our new house in Frederick Place and a little of our
life there. The next six years of my life formed the most stable
period of my childhood. Frederick Place was a street of superior two-
storied terrace houses – superior in that the front doors and porches were
separated from the pavement by narrow strips of garden, frequently
flagged or dominated by a shrub and a row of iron railings.

No. 88 was typical. The floor of the small porch was of a pristine
whiteness and I remember my mother, like all her neighbours, on her
hands and knees holystoning it once a week. Inside the hall there were
doors leading to the front room and to the living room, and then you
passed through a dark room with a kitchen-range into a small scullery.
Upstairs there were three rooms; the front room was my parents'
bedroom, the middle one was my bedroom, and the third at the top of the
stairs had been converted into a bathroom. The white enamelled bath
crouched on its iron paws, and over it hung a large copper geyser for
heating the bath water. There was no lavatory (which we all called the
'lav'); this was outside in the back yard, built on to the scullery and not a
place to linger in the winter. The house was lit by gas. Our front room was
rarely used except at Christmas or when we had visitors; it was always
referred to as the 'front room' and never the parlour or sitting room, and
certainly not the lounge. There was not a great deal of room in which to
manoeuvre, given the upholstered three-piece suite, oak sideboard, gate-
legged table and wind-up gramophone cabinet. The latter was stained and
polished to resemble mahogany, had two carved doors and mock-cabriole
legs, and was my mother's pride and joy. Presumably, my father bought it
at my mother's insistence but it was very rarely used, mainly, I suppose,

because we had so few records. Perhaps, as so often happens, enthusiasm evaporated with acquisition, but I cannot remember any records being bought after the first couple of months. After a dainty tea, visitors were usually regaled with selections from Rose Marie. I was more interested in the two floppy discs we acquired. They were white and flexible and made of what appeared to be celluloid. I think they must have been either demonstration or advertising records but I have never come across anything like them since.

I cannot understand why we did not have a piano. I am sure my father could have afforded one, certainly a second-hand one. This was a pity because my mother, despite no formal musical training, was one of those fortunate people able to play by ear. Before she was married, she occasionally used to deputise at a cinema in Brighton for the pianist who accompanied the silent films. When we visited friends or relatives who had a piano she was always encouraged to play, and I was astonished and impressed when she sat down at the piano. Then, without any music or preamble, she would proceed to strike up popular tunes of the day. Although I was conscious of music from an early age and later became a choirboy, I regret very much that I never learned to read music or play an instrument. Perhaps it was just as well because I expect I would have resisted the idea anyway, and I found later on that I had little sense of rhythm.

Our domestic life centred round the living room. Here we sat, ate, read, relaxed, listened to the wireless and played cards and board games. Here we also entertained casual visitors and relatives. On the pine table, with its green chenille cloth removed, my mother did her ironing and made cakes and pastry. My father usually did his odd jobs upon it when it was too cold or wet to go down to the shed and this was sometimes a source of some friction. When my mother mildly complained about sawdust on the floor and dust upon the furniture, my father retorted that he could not be expected to do jobs indoors without making a bit of a mess. In his later years, when his interest in doing odd jobs about the house rapidly declined, he would always blame this upon my mother's 'going on' at him in past years about the mess he made. From the living room a window looked out on to the back yard and to the garden beyond it.

The narrow room with the kitchen-range in it was rarely used. It had a table and a couple of chairs but it was more a passage through to the scullery rather than a room. I cannot remember the range ever being lit or the room used as a kitchen. My mother black-leaded the range religiously but since the room was dark and cheerless, I rarely played on the table there.

My mother cooked on a gas stove in the scullery. This small room also contained a shallow stone sink (later to have an Ascot gas water heater fixed above it), a copper built into one corner and a door leading to the coalhole in another. In pre-Ascot days, if you wanted hot water you had to put a kettle on the stove. When we first went to no. 88 my mother used the copper for heating the water for the weekly Monday wash. Everyone washed on Mondays regardless of the weather. I remember her vividly, scrubbing away at the sink at the clothes on her washboard and stirring the whites in the copper with her special copper-stick amid clouds of steam. She used to rinse all her washing by hand, sheets as well, and then, when I was home, I used to help her by feeding them through the mangle.

Our tiny back yard was quite large enough for a small boy to play cricket. My father always came home from the office for his dinner and

The young cricketer.

afterwards, if the weather was fine, we had a brief game. The wicket was chalked on the wall beneath the living room window and my parents took it in turns to bowl a tennis ball underarm to me while the other fielded. I was not allowed to hit the ball in the air (windows!) or back over their heads into the garden (flowers!); instead I had to concentrate on slogging it low and straight, because on the leg-side was a wooden fence dividing us from our neighbours, the Pophams.

At the end of the yard there were three stone steps up to the garden. My father used the top step to sharpen the carving knife on Sunday mornings in readiness for our roast dinner. To one side of the narrow garden was an herbaceous border, while the other was given over to a small lawn and flowerbeds. Beyond this lawn was the vegetable patch where my father grew lettuces, carrots, runner beans, potatoes and cabbages. At the bottom of the garden was my father's shed. Most men like to have a shed to potter about in away from domestic pressures and my father spent many happy hours in his at the weekends. He built it himself out of scrap timber and it was large enough to hold a workbench plus the lawn mower, garden tools, deckchairs and items waiting patiently to be repaired. More importantly, it gave me a private place to play in when it was too cold or wet to play outside. Both my parents were interested in gardening; they chose bedding plants together and bought flower seeds from Woolworths. One of my happiest memories is of them working amiably together in the garden on warm summer evenings.

There were no trees or shrubs in our garden but the Pophams had a splendid poplar at the bottom of theirs. They also had two sons. We only saw Harold, the elder, now and again because he was married and lived in Nottingham. Will, the younger son, was a pleasant-looking bachelor regarded by everybody as 'artistic'. I think he worked as a draughtsman in the Arsenal but I cannot be certain. Unusually for those days and for his class, he used to go abroad for his summer holidays, walking and climbing in the Alps. Occasionally, in summer he used to appear in the garden in lederhosen and Tyrolean hat with a coil of rope around his shoulders. To the amusement of his neighbours working in their gardens, he would then rope up and attack the poplar. I only actually went into the Popham's house on two or three occasions, though I was always asking old Mrs Popham – a short, squat, heavy, puffing sort of lady – to throw my ball back from her yard. Once, Will did invite me into their front room, which I realised was his own sanctum, to show me his collection of butterflies. He had case upon mahogany case of beautifully mounted specimens but it struck me as a rather sterile pursuit.

Frederick Place was built across the hill that sloped down to Woolwich Arsenal and the Thames, with St James' Church at one end and Sandy Hill

Lane at the other. It was bisected by Bloomfield Road, a main road that carried the 53 bus service. On our side of Frederick Place at the corner of Bloomfield Road stood a public house, the Freemason's Arms, with Webb's off-licence opposite. On the other side of Bloomfield Road was the Co-op (the Royal Arsenal Co-operative Society). This had several departments, including a butcher and a greengrocer, and since it was set a long way back from the road, it provided a useful forecourt. Higher up Bloomfield Road, on the corner of St James' Place, was the Post Office, which also sold cakes, and a few doors along were the newsagents where we bought our comics. Opposite were the local chemist and Finer's, the tailor, and facing them across Bloomfield Road was our local fish and chip shop. This was the sum of the shops in our neighbourhood, except for Serjeants, the sweet shop, and Payne's, the barbers, a few yards below the Freemason's Arms.

Like all my friends, unless it was raining or cold or I was reading or amusing myself indoors, I played outside in the street. This meant our half of Frederick Place and 'the block', the rectangular area bounded by Bloomfield Road and Burrage Road running downhill and St James' Place and Frederick Place running across. It measured 132 yards by 85 – I paced it out once. This was our territory. Occasionally, we made brief forays into neighbouring streets but it is remarkable how little in ordinary play we strayed from Frederick Place. I remember that one summer there was a sudden craze for running laps round the block. Night after night after tea we used to hurl ourselves, panting and wet with perspiration, round the block, quarter-mile lap after quarter-mile lap to see who could run the furthest. At last, one or two of the older boys who had joined us became alarmed at our state and made us stop. 'Us' was not a gang as such. It was a spasmodic coming-together of small boys, rarely all at the same time, for various activities – Alan Peters, Vicky Arrowsmith, Paul Cummings, Derek Sargent. Occasionally we would be joined by one or more Fox Hill friends who lived a few streets away; they would stay with us for a brief while and then drift away.

Some time after we were established in Frederick Place, I decided to become a cub. The cub pack met in the large hall of the Methodist church in Herbert Road. On the wall hung a portrait of the Chief Scout, Lord Baden-Powell, hero of Mafeking in the Boer War, who founded the Scouting movement in 1908 and in the same year published his seminal book *Scouting for Boys*. The Chief Scout, wearing his distinctive wide-brimmed hat, gazed down benignly upon our activities. After a few weeks preparation, I made my promises at a rather solemn ceremony and was formally inducted. I now had my uniform and for several years I enjoyed being a cub very much. I liked the parades and the rituals; I dob-dob-dobbed with the rest of them in response to Akela's dyb-dyb-dybbing, though it was not until many years later that I realised what dyb and dob actually stood for. I savoured the faintly military air and the competitive games, which were different from those we played in 'drill' at school; I liked the simple woodcraft we were taught, the knots and the acquisition of badges proudly sewn on our jerseys. I also enjoyed the hierarchical structure and opportunities for advancement to a 'seconder' or even to the giddy heights of a 'sixer'.

In the 1930s there was virtually no motor traffic along Frederick Place, so 'Last Across' was rarely played. No one in our road had a car and there were few in the neighbourhood; there were naturally no garages either. Buses, together with the occasional light van and the odd car, ran down Bloomfield Road, but there was little to disturb our play except for the daily visit of Meckiff the baker. I think he was the only tradesman at that time to deliver by van, although, in his case, it was not so much a van as a succession of ancient saloon cars with the loaves stacked all over the leather-upholstered back seat and sometimes in the boot. He once told my father that he never reckoned to pay more than 35s for a car – and I can well believe it.

Meckiff was a cheerful, friendly soul, the uncle of my close friend Georgie Gibson, and thus well disposed towards me. He baked his bread at the back of his shop in Raglan Road, which was both bakery and dairy and smelt like a country kitchen. His wife, May, sold bread and dispensed milk from the churn with a copper dipper and kept the shop spotless. She polished the row of brass weights by the scales till they shone like gold and scrubbed the wooden counters so vigorously that you could feel the raised grain under your fingertips, much like the seam on a cricket ball.

Our milk (from United Dairies), like our coal, was delivered by horse-drawn cart. Coal, I think, was 1s 3d per hundredweight. Our coalmen wore blackened leather hoods reaching down their backs. Easing the hundredweight sacks onto their shoulders from the wagon, they carried the sacks straight through the house into the scullery and emptied them into the coalhole with a great roar. If we happened to be out during a storm and it thundered, my father used to look up at the heavens and say, 'Ah, that's God getting his coal in'. Meat was delivered by the traditional butcher's boy, riding a bicycle with the deep metal carrier on the front and a plate with the butcher's name and address on it set in the frame beneath the crossbar.

As far as I was concerned, the advantage of horse-drawn carts (now that I had given up stampeding horses) was the rich harvest they yielded. My interest in this waxed and waned, usually being triggered off by the sight of a pile of steaming manure in the road. When the mood took me, I seized the coal shovel and a bucket, raced out and filled the bucket to the brim. I then went up and down the street, asking our neighbours if they wanted a bucket of manure, price one penny. Among ourselves we called it 'dung' but I tried hard to remember to call it 'manure' on the sales side. There always seemed to be a ready market for it, but I found it difficult to develop the business. As soon as one of my friends spotted what I was doing he would be out of his house in a flash with his bucket and shovel and the roads round the block would be swept clear. As in life, one had to seize the moment.

SEVEN

Close Relatives;
Closet Relations

'Hope, like the gleaming taper's light,
Adorns and cheers our way . . .'

The Captivity, Goldsmith

When we first moved to Frederick Place, I realised that just round the corner at 186 Burrage Road lived our distant cousins, the Bristows. They must have moved there from Paget Rise a little before we did, probably following Arthur's death, of which I remember nothing. Their house was a largish, three-storied, semi-detached affair where you went down a couple of stairs from the front hall into the living room. Beyond the living room was the kitchen, which also contained a bath kept boarded over when not in use. A back door led out through the yard to the outside lavatory and to a long narrow garden with a row of apple trees running down the middle of it. This arrangement made it difficult for anyone to go to the lavatory or cook a meal if one of the family was having a bath. Baths, therefore, had to be carefully planned. It did not strike me as strange that so large a house had no proper bathroom. Bathrooms were rare at that time among our circle; our lavatories were outside and bathrooms were essentially baths fitted into a spare bedroom or into the kitchen.

Because their house was lit by gas at this time, there was no light in their outside lavatory. Members of the family, when the spirit moved them, had to sally forth into the dark with a candlestick (if wishing to read) or a torch. Under these circumstances it was difficult to disguise one's business, if I may put it like that; everyone knew where you were going and what for. My male relatives would make off with the paper; have a smoke and catch up on the news while 'awaiting the call', as they phrased it. Eric was a great one for disappearing into the lavatory for hours on end with a book or paper and his family pulled his leg endlessly.

If he went out during the evening equipped with candlestick and reading matter, his going was accompanied by remarks such as 'He's gone for the night then' or 'We shan't be seeing him for a couple of hours.'

We were in much the same position at home. Also, since no one in their right mind relished going outside to the lavatory in the middle of the night, especially in winter, we, like other families, kept chamber pots (always called 'pos' and the source of many jokes and much merriment) under our beds. Every morning, the contents were poured into the slop pail, which in its turn was emptied down the pan outside.

Among my parents and relatives there seemed a curious obsession with lavatories and bowel movements. The latter loomed large in their lives and it certainly played a significant part in my father's regimen. Whether this pre-occupation with their bowels was passed on from father to son, or a symptom of an unbalanced diet (they ate little fruit and less salad), a relic of army life, or simply a class thing, I do not know. Every day of his life my father took a dose of senna pods, supplementing this, if he wanted a stronger aperient, with a piece of the dark-chocolate-seeming Ex-lax. Not only could visits to the lavatory not be concealed, in our family they were announced and the results discussed with a certain relish. After a 'good turn-out' or a 'good start to the day', a sense of accomplishment, a feeling of well-being pervaded the house. In connection with this, I remember my father, on the rare occasions when he broke wind, chanting:

'Where-e'er you be, let your wind go free;
In church or chapel let it rattle.'

This did not amuse my mother. 'Oh, Jack!' she would sigh, 'not in front of the boy.' 'Oh, it's only a bit of fun,' my father would cheerfully reply.

While dealing with the mysteries of the toilet, perhaps I should say something about bathing. Although we possessed a bath we only bathed once a week; to bath more frequently, as Marjorie did, was considered both eccentric and extravagant. We performed our weekly ritual on Friday or Saturday night, lighting the gas under the copper geyser and waiting patiently for the water to get hot. Friday night was often jokingly referred to as 'Amami night'. Like those other slogans of the 1930s – 'Did you MacLean your teeth today?' and 'Guinness is good for you' – it is deeply buried in one's consciousness. On the morning after our baths, we changed our clothes so that they would be ready for washing on Monday. My parents never varied this routine of one bath per week, regardless of season or activity, but despite it, my father never smelt of stale perspiration, even in high summer. About him hung a pleasant aroma consisting of St Julien pipe tobacco and Yardley's Brilliantine. Every morning after shaving at the sink and having a wash ('sloosh', he called it), he would take a little grease from the oval tin that was part of the sink furniture and rub it into his thick, dark hair. Much to my mother's irritation, he always shaved at the sink while she was trying to get the breakfast. Even when he acquired a house with a proper bathroom several years later, he still insisted on shaving and washing at the sink in the kitchen.

If outside lavatories were daunting places in winter, our bedrooms and bathrooms were only several degrees better. We had, of course, no central heating; there were small black-leaded grates in the bedrooms but fires were only lit in them in case of illness. Going to bed in winter was a penance to be accomplished as rapidly as possible. I often used to undress by the fire in the living room and then race up the stairs and jump into bed. When I awoke in the morning there would be rime or ice on the inside of my window, and washing in the unheated bathroom became something of a lick and a promise. Later, when electricity was installed, we sometimes brought the electric fire up into the bedroom to dress or undress by, and often into the bathroom. But such occasions were rare. We accepted that bedroom conditions were like this; it was nothing out of the ordinary and, in any case, old habits die hard. I slept warm and cosy in my feather bed; on bitterly cold nights I sank deep into this until only the top of my head was visible over the blankets and eiderdown. With the bed already warmed by a hot-water bottle (stone was going out, rubber coming in) I was, to use a familiar phrase, 'as snug as a bug in a rug'. On light evenings in summer I read in bed but I never attempted to do so in winter. Apart from the difficulty of keeping your hands warm, there was always, in the absence of bedside lamps, the thought at the back of your mind that when you had finished reading and were ready to settle down, you would have to hop out of bed onto the cold lino to switch the light off by the door.

I also suffered in winter from chapped legs. We all wore short trousers, of course; in fact, I wore short trousers for the first two years at my grammar school. Despite wearing a mackintosh in cold or wet weather, what with the wind and the rain and the rubbing of my trousers, the skin on the inside of my thighs became red and inflamed and remained so for some time, although I smeared ointment on them night and morning. While on the subject of minor bodily ills, throughout the year I seemed, like my friends, to have scabs on my knees. These came in the main from tripping over the pavement, falling while messing about and coming a cropper on my skates. As one grows older, other parts of the body take the strain – backs, shoulders, hamstrings – but knees are the most prominent and susceptible parts of a boy's anatomy. I confess (this book has many awful admissions) that I used to enjoy picking at my scabs and easing them off before they were properly ready to come away. My mother used to chant Arthur Askey's line at me, 'It will never get well if you pick it', and this catchphrase is still used within the family.

From time to time, we went round to Burrage Road to have tea with the family. Old Uncle Mark presided at the head of the table, drinking his tea from his saucer and staining his white moustache brown. The front room downstairs was his sitting room and he and my father played crib in the evening. I learned how to play by sitting quietly on the red plush sofa and drinking in such mysteries as 'fifteen two, fifteen four, a pair's six and three are nine' or 'four for a flush and one for his nob, five'. Uncle Mark often used to come round to us on Saturday evenings to play crib with my father, whom he genuinely liked and regarded as his protégé. More to the point, he enjoyed the Welsh rarebit my mother always made for him afterwards.

The Bristows of Burrage Road were great card players, like the Potter family and ourselves. As I grew older I loved going round there with my

The Potter family in 1938.

parents and while my father was seriously engaged with Uncle Mark in the front room, my mother and I, with Auntie Elsie, Peter, Leslie, Eric and Marjorie (if they were in), would sit round the big living-room table and play the old family card games. We played knockout whist, sevens, chase the ace, rummy, newmarket (with matches) and occasionally, mainly for my benefit, Happy Families and uproarious games of Pit.

Although I was cocooned in a loving home and cradled, as it were, in a web of family relationships, I think it was on occasions like this that I dimly began to appreciate what I was missing as an only child. Not that for one moment did I feel a sense of loss or deprivation, for I cannot remember even feeling particularly lonely or bored. But increasingly I began to envy those friends of mine who had brothers and sisters to play with, especially on holiday, and I always enjoyed the warmth of their family life.

By the mid-1930s, Marjorie had grown into a tall, blonde, attractive girl and would be married before the war. Eric was working as a clerk in the Woolwich Equitable Building Society, where he was to remain until his retirement. Leslie, suffering for years from asthma and eczema, was an engineering craftsman. Sadly, he was to lose an eye in an accident at his bench a little later and to die in early middle age. All three were very kind to me as a child; there were always presents at Christmas and on my birthday, and odd pennies and ice creams in between. There was no one, however, quite like Peter. Because he was a couple of years older than me, he had a quite different circle of friends and although we both attended Fox Hill together at one stage, he was a 'big boy' and we saw little of each other. I worshipped him from a distance – to play cards with him or, very occasionally, play ball with him, or pelt each other with windfalls in his garden, was heaven.

Now and again, when we went round the corner to no. 186 we found Elsie's brother, Stan, there with his wife, Lily, and their daughter, Lorna. Following some preliminary manoeuvring and army banter, Stan would launch into his stories. After the First World War he had become a commercial traveller in furnishing fabrics for a firm in the City, roving all over the eastern counties and East Midlands. He was a wonderful raconteur, a natural storyteller with a gift for characterisation and an eye for detail, drawing on the ups and downs of life in shops, stores and commercial hotels. His two great loves were music, especially church music, and cricket. When he was working in East Anglia he arranged his calls so that he could finish in Cambridge and slip into King's College Chapel for evensong. Whenever he found himself in a cathedral city or near a church of some musical distinction, he would contrive to enjoy the stimulus and solace of church music. His usual mode of address, even to me, was 'old man'. So he would come out with a comment to my father such as, 'Jack, old man, I finished up in Bury St Edmunds last week. I saw they were doing Stanford in B Flat. Marvellous!' I remember that when he did not quite catch what you said, he would cock his head on one side, cup his hand to his better ear and enquire, 'What was that you said old man?'

Sadly, his enjoyment of music was marred by the damage done to his hearing during the war. However, later on, he had one of the very first NHS hearing aids with wires leading to a small control box on his chest, looking for all the world like a bus conductor with his ticket machine. Fiddling about to tune this produced squeals, shrieks and anguished expressions on his face. Then, as he succeeded in fixing it, a beatific smile spread slowly over his face. For many years he was a season-ticket holder and highly critical devotee of Essex County Cricket Club. Living in Ilford he was within easy reach of their grounds and I sometimes suspect his calls in the county in summer were built around the Essex fixture list.

Although I always ate a good tea at Auntie Elsie's, I suddenly became finicky about food at home. I must have driven my mother, who was a good plain cook, to despair. My father liked traditional food. He was basically a meat-and-two-veg man and was not interested in what he referred to as 'messed-up food'. He was fortunate in having a wife who was not only a very competent housewife and manager but who presented him day after day with a variety of hot, wholesome dishes for his dinner. Roasts, pies, stews, steak and chops were varied with fish, sheep's head (ugh!) and liver and bacon, and there was often a tasty snack for his tea.

To return to my muttons, I do not know why I was faddy or awkward. I suspect it was because I was never made to finish my food before being allowed to get down from the table. Thus I either left what I did not fancy or ate as much, or as little, of what I liked. Those were the days of cheap food and I am ashamed (and full of regret!) when I think back to the dishes, particularly the meat, I used to spurn. Matters were not improved by my being painfully thin and having little appetite. I suppose I must have eaten something to keep the flame alive. I liked eggs, cheese, tinned fruit salad and puddings so I did not starve, but mine was a bizarre and meagre diet. At one difficult stage, I seemed to exist almost entirely on Oxo and pork brawn. My mother, at her wits' end, sent me down daily to the Co-op on the corner for a quarter of pork brawn. I was struck with the dexterity of the assistant who sliced the brawn so thinly, slid it onto a sheet of greaseproof paper, wrapped it in coarse white paper and slapped it on top of the glass shelf above the counter with a flourish. I also liked to watch him cutting cheese with a wire and toggle, and I admired the precision with which he could produce exactly half a pound of cheddar or a quarter of gorgonzola. I went off pork brawn as suddenly as I conceived a passion for it and I have never eaten it since.

As in most households, my mother had a weekly routine for housework, shopping, washing and ironing, and this was echoed by a similar rhythm in her cooking. On Sundays we always had a roast dinner with all the trimmings and this was the culinary high point for us, as it was for most friends and relatives. On Mondays we had the joint cold with either boiled potatoes or bubble and squeak – Sunday's potatoes fried up with the leftover vegetables. Then, on Tuesdays, the remains of the joint would be done up in some way, either as mince or shepherd's pie, or mince with curry powder added. I did not look forward to Tuesdays. For the remaining four days my mother drew on her repertoire.

She always served a proper pudding at dinner. These were the puddings of my parents' Edwardian childhoods. My mother produced two types of suet pudding: plain ones steamed in a cloth and eaten with golden syrup, and spotted dick, a suet pudding studded with currants. I particularly liked a treacle sponge turned out from a basin, which we called 'Aunt Nellie Pudding', though I do not know why. There were also bread-and-butter puddings, jam and treacle tarts (we liked treacle!), and a range of pies – apple, plum, rhubarb and blackberry and apple. All these I enjoyed but I drew the line at stewed fruit. Of course, many of these puddings could only be made when the fruit was in season. I remember how my parents used to look forward to the coming of certain fruits such as Victoria plums and raspberries. Seasonal, too, were the vegetables we ate. We enjoyed lettuce, beetroot, peas, beans and tomatoes in the summer, but once that was over and winter was upon us we mainly ate cabbage, Brussels sprouts, swede, parsnips, carrots or tinned peas with our meat.

We drank tea for breakfast, water with our dinner, tea at teatime and either cocoa or Ovaltine before going to bed. Coffee was not drunk except when we had visitors. Favoured visitors had percolated coffee; the more mundane got Camp Coffee from the bottle. I rarely had any.

'Tea' was neither 'high', 'polite afternoon' nor 'knife and fork'. We had it about 6 p.m. when my father came home from the office and it normally consisted of bread and butter with jam, Heinz sandwich spread, cheese, lemon curd or paste to go with it. There was always a little jar of Shippam's bloater paste, salmon and shrimp paste, fish paste, meat paste or ham and tongue paste on the table. I did not care for paste, especially in sandwiches, but I would eat meat paste smeared with mustard when the mood seized me. This was followed by homemade cake or, at the weekends, a plate of 'fancies'. In my perverse way, and with my sweet tooth, I naturally preferred shop cakes.

Tea became a much more expansive meal when we had visitors. We hardly ever entertained anyone at lunchtime, which we called 'dinnertime'; friends and relatives were invited to tea. Besides the large plate of bread and butter, plus things to spread on it, there was cheese and celery and my mother made sandwiches, usually cucumber (which I disliked), backed up by egg, sardine or tomato. After this came tinned fruit salad with tinned cream or jelly and blancmange. It would all be rounded off with a Victoria sponge, fruit cake and fancies. In summer, the sandwiches were omitted in favour of cold ham and salad, the latter always including hard-boiled eggs and beetroot.

Our visitors were almost always relatives, rarely friends. In fact, I cannot readily think of more than one couple other than relatives who came to the house for tea. Perhaps this was because in their Frederick Place days, my parents knew few married couples they would consider inviting round. My mother regarded herself as 'rather reserved' and there was no working-class camaraderie, no 'cup of sugar' syndrome and no neighbours popping in for a chat or a cup of tea in our street. Similarly, few relatives ever stayed the night; in our circle, one went for the day. The exception was Nana, who stayed with us for several days when she came up from Brighton.

When we had visitors for the evening I would reluctantly go to bed before they left. I remember lying in bed, warm and sleepy, listening through my half-open door to the hum of conversation downstairs. From time to time, this was punctuated by bursts of laughter and I longed to know what they were saying and what they were laughing at. This is one of the emotive memories of childhood. It was similar to the experience of being unwell and lying in bed listening to the sounds of the house – faint footsteps in the hall, the murmur of the wireless, the clink of cups and plates, the soft closing of a door. From outside there filtered in cries from the street, the noise of a rare passing car and, on summer evenings, voices of neighbours in their gardens and the drowsy whirring of a lawn mower in the distance.

Fortunately, I was rarely ill and never had to go into hospital. I had all the usual childish ailments but once the initial unpleasantness was over, I rather enjoyed the aftermath of being unwell. My mother fussed over me, lit a fire in my bedroom if it was cold, and pandered to my curious tastes in food with light meals delicately presented. In the evenings she brought me a hot drink and sat on the bottom of my bed and chatted. When it was time for me to settle down, she plumped up my pillows, tucked me up, kissed me goodnight and quietly went downstairs, leaving the bedroom door open in case I wanted anything during the night. It is a good thing to spoil a sick child a little; I was spoilt something rotten anyway.

EIGHT

UNDER TAURUS

'For when the One Great Scorer comes
To write against your name,
He marks – not that you won or lost –
But how you played the game.'

Alumnus Football, Grantland Rice

In September 1933 I started at Fox Hill Junior School. The school stood almost at the bottom of a steep slope at the end of Plumstead Common Road – Woolwich is a hilly place! – about half a mile from my home. The headmaster was Cyril Bull, a handsome, sturdily built man. He was a strong personality, dominant but not domineering, who was active in

Fox Hill School.

The school cricket XI with Cyril Bull.

public life in Woolwich. He was greatly interested in sport and helped to found the Woolwich School Sports Association. He could always be seen at football and cricket matches, boxing tournaments and swimming galas, helping with the organisation and, above all, encouraging the competitors. He was a magistrate for many years and a prominent figure on local hospital committees. His generous nature, good humour, and willingness to listen and to help made him highly valued by all those who came into contact with him. He was always smartly turned out; he habitually wore a black coat and striped trousers, often with a bow tie. He also had a fondness for buttonholes. In summer it was a rose from his garden in Grosmount Road; in winter he favoured a carnation.

The boys who attended Fox Hill owe him a considerable debt. I think he influenced me more than anyone else I encountered during my school and university life. He was strict but we were never afraid of him and it was a happy and well-ordered school. Certain remarks he made throw light upon his character. I remember particularly, when he read out at prayers the names of the boys chosen to play for the school cricket side, how he would stress: 'Now, you boys have been chosen to play for the school. It's an honour. And you will turn up, rain, hail or snow. No matter what happens, you must turn up.' We never let him down. He often came to watch us when we were playing. His maxim imprinted on us was 'always play the game', a simple moral precept we carried with us afterwards and repeated in our turn.

The school had been built in 1881. The front door, reserved for the use of staff, was approached by a steep flight of steps; boys had to enter by an alley at the side which led into the playground. Whatever the weather, we were not allowed to enter the school until the master on duty came out and blew his whistle. When we heard it, we stood stock-still; a second blast and we fell in by classes to be marched indoors.

As in so many late Victorian schools, there were classrooms – in this case five – opening into a small hall. The hall was fitted with folding dividing doors so that it could become two classrooms in an emergency. There were few emergencies under Cyril Bull and I can hardly recall the doors ever being closed. At one end of the hall was the platform, with the head's desk on it and the piano upon which C.B. Walkem (known as 'Paddy' on account of his quick temper) played the hymns at prayers. When Paddy was away, Cyril Bull played for us – head teachers could and did in those days! It was Cyril Bull who sparked off my interest in music.

Fox Hill School form photograph.

58

Sometimes we would file into the hall for prayers and find a record being played on the radiogram. On rare occasions, after prayers, the head would tell us to sit and then say a few words about the music he was going to play. The first pieces of serious music I heard (apart from the overture to 'William Tell', the *pièce de resistance* of the R.A. Band) was Grieg's 'In the Hall of the Mountain King' from his *Peer Gynt Suite* – to which we did a kind of seated jig, with much shaking of our shoulders – and the haunting barcarolle from *The Tales of Hoffman*.

Apart from morning prayers, the hall was used for singing lessons, for the Scholarship examination and for 'drill' when it was too miserable to go outside in the playground. Along one wall were individual framed photographs of those boys who had passed the 'Scholarship' and had gone on to various London grammar schools. The point was not lost upon us and Cyril Bull used to indicate them and tell the top class, 'I want to see photographs of some of you on that wall. You can do it if you try.' In due course some of us obliged.

It was an enlightened school in many ways with an emphasis on striving to do your best, on getting on and doing well in life, on loyalty, and not letting the school down. Boys were hardly ever caned or struck by the teachers and the head only very rarely caned boys publicly. This was invariably when boys had let the school down by bad behaviour outside. We always knew what was afoot when we filed into the hall in the morning and saw the cane lying across the head's desk. We grinned at each other and hugged ourselves in anticipation. After prayers the boy would be called up to the platform. There would be a brief homily from Cyril Bull, followed by a few strokes of the cane and the offender returned in tears to his place wringing his hand. The scene ended with Cyril Bull threatening to do the same to any boy found committing that particular offence again. It put the fear of God into us.

When I started at Fox Hill, I was put in Mr Codrington's class. His son, Roy, who later became a friend of mine, was also in the class, which I felt was something of an embarrassment for him. Every morning we started the day with a session of times-tables. These we chanted, from the two- to the twelve-times-table, a piping, pounding rhythm that still rings in the ears over the years. As the months passed and we became more secure in our tables, so the drills would become more selective; perhaps the six-times- and the nine-times-tables only. These were reinforced by questions rapidly fired round the class in turn. I soaked all this up and became quick and accurate at mental arithmetic and sums. We spent much time learning to write a clear, cursive hand using the standard wooden pen and steel nib. Reading round the class was accompanied by spelling rules and spelling tests and then, suddenly, we were on the threshold of composition.

As we moved up the school our spelling tests, English exercises and sums were always marked and the marks disclosed round the class. There were also formal tests at the end of each term in the full range of subjects. We were even marked for drill, though fortunately not for singing. It was an excellent preparation for the scholarship examination, now looming on our boyish horizons. The competitive spirit was fostered by teaching methods which set boy against boy, one half of the class against the other, or – as we had no house system – lines of desks competing against other lines of desks. We accepted this as quite natural and we became very excited after the end of term exams when our class teacher read out the marks for the various subjects. Much feverish addition and comparison of totals went on to find out who had come top.

There was great competition for the post of class monitor. Two reliable boys were chosen by the class teacher to carry out such desirable tasks as filling up the inkwells from the large brown earthenware bottle in the cupboard, giving out pens and rulers, and handing out and collecting textbooks and exercise books. A few minutes before playtime in the morning, the monitors would go out and collect the crate of bottles of free milk for the class, one third of a pint per boy. Ah, to be a monitor was a highly coveted position.

As the years passed, it gradually began to dawn on me that I was among the brightest boys in my class, though we did not use the word 'bright' – we said 'clever'. The work came easily to me and I enjoyed the competitive element like most clever boys. I was not considered a 'swot', then or later, since swots were pale, studious boys who wore glasses and were useless at games. I enjoyed games and drill was my favourite lesson. Being quick and agile, I looked forward to this all week and I prayed that it would not rain on that particular day. If our class became noisy, the threat of cancelling drill was enough to bring us to heel.

We took off our jackets, ties and pullovers in the cloakroom, changed into plimsolls (we were not allowed to do drill in ordinary shoes) and formed up in line in the playground in four teams with the team leader at the front. Each team wore a different coloured sash and we performed a programme of Swedish exercises as a warm-up. This was followed by several traditional line games, such as tunnel ball or potato racing, highly competitive and played with a ferocious intensity. Finally, as a treat, we used to round off the lesson by playing a modified version of netball, hilarious versions of 'He', or throwing a football to hit the boy in the circle below the knees.

One incident sticks in my mind. One sunny morning when I was about ten and we were due for drill, I discovered at breakfast that I had left my plimsolls at a relative's house. Disaster! No plimsolls, no drill. Then I had a brainwave. I rushed upstairs, hauled out the holiday trunk from under my parents' bed, and pulled out my blue and white rubber beach shoes. Relieved, I set out for school without a second thought. The time for drill arrived. I changed into my beach shoes and slipped out into the playground. I was surprised, then embarrassed, by my reception. My classmates pointed fingers of scorn and sniggered; several openly jeered. I had never experienced anything like this before. My class teacher called me over and asked what I was wearing and 'what did I think this was?' I explained my problem and how I had overcome it. Instead of being congratulated, as I half-expected, he pursed his lips and grudgingly admitted me back into the line. I was close to tears and bitterly ashamed. The drill period seemed endless until at last I could tear off my shoes and bury them in my satchel.

An experience like this cut deep. I had done something in my innocence and eagerness that had offended the herd and for the first time in my life I felt a disturbing sense of isolation. I was never a stubborn or difficult child and I happily accepted authority and discipline. But inside me that day was sown a seed that developed into a pre-disposition to take and hold a minority view, a subconscious refusal to accept the majority view and to defy the mob. This attitude was certainly not born out of either perverseness or a reluctance to conform, but rather from a certain sense of injustice, allied to a growing consciousness of individuality. Being an only child probably had something to do with it, too.

In one corner of our playground stood the dustbins. These were generally ignored except after a fall of snow when they were traditionally formed into a barricade by the top class and defended against the rest of the school. When I was in the top class we used to arrive early to make a pile of snowballs to fight off the other boys as they arrived. This was great fun and usually ended in us being overwhelmed when we ran out of snow. I never derived much pleasure from our other winter pastime, the long slide made across the frozen playground. For some reason I was never very good at sliding. I seemed unable to achieve the proper balance and I usually ended up on my backside. Once or twice, when my feet shot away from me, I came down hard on the back of my head. This was painful and led to my renouncing sliding forever.

Although I had little interest in what was going on nationally, I was very much aware in 1936 of the major domestic upheaval of the decade. This was the romance between our new but never crowned king, Edward VIII, and the famous Mrs Simpson, culminating in the abdication crisis. During the height of the drama, we trotted to and from school (we went everywhere at the double in those days of endless stamina) singing:

'Who's that coming down the street?
Mrs Simpson and her sweet.
She's been married once before,
Now she's knocking on Edward's door.'

And then, later on:

'Hark! The herald angels sing
Mrs Simpson's pinched our King.'

The following year we had the excitement of the coronation of King George VI and Queen Elizabeth and every boy was presented with a commemorative beaker from the LCC. I did not like the beaker very much and nor did anyone else. I preferred the proper mug we received in May 1935 for the Silver Jubilee of King George V and Queen Mary. Besides, on

Silver Jubilee commemorative photograph and card, 1935.

that occasion we were also given an attractive tin full of sweets with a picture of the King and Queen on it. I saw pictures in the papers of the children's street parties being held in parts of London, with bunting strung across the street and tables running down the middle laden with food and soft drinks. Naturally, there were no street parties where I lived. I was told that only happened in poor areas. Children there seemed to have all the fun on such occasions.

I flourished in the top class under the strict eye of Mr W.A. Williams, the senior teacher. 'Wally', as we called him, was tall, thin and silver-haired, and he must have been in his fifties then. He was a fine, experienced teacher who worked us hard but knew when to unwind. Sometimes towards the end of Friday afternoons, if we had been working well, he would read us a story. He read Kipling's *Just So Stories* and *The Jungle Book* (Rikki Tikki Tavi was a favourite) and Stephen Leacock's *Sunshine Sketches of a Little Town*. From such tiny acorns . . .

The school competed in the Woolwich & District annual school sports. I was not a fast runner then and did nothing of note until my last summer when I entered the potato race. True to form, I finished a poor third in the semi-final and had little hope of achieving even that in the final. Yet, reaching new heights of nimbleness, I won the final by yards and thus became the under-11 champion potato racer of Woolwich & District. I stepped up to receive my prize, which turned out to be a splendid leather picnic case filled with bakelite plates, cups and saucers, etc. I later found one in a store priced at 7s 6d, a lot of money in those days. This case lasted the family for years, which was just as well, as I never won another prize at athletics, where mere fleetness of foot was prized above agility.

Every summer the staff organised a school journey for the boys in the two senior classes to Sandown on the Isle of Wight. We went for a fortnight in July and stayed in the Trouville Hotel on the front. Cyril Bull, Sid Woolley, Eric Gimson and their wives usually accompanied us. Hardly any of us had ever been inside a proper hotel before, let alone spent a holiday in one, so the summers of '36 and '37 were a new experience for us.

Most of our time was spent on the beach. At that time there was a long drop from the promenade to the shingle below and my chunky friend, Firebrace (inevitably known as 'Fireplace'), suddenly shot to fame for his daring in jumping casually down to the stones below with a thud that made his teeth rattle. Cyril Bull was very adept at exciting our interest when he sensed that the momentum of the holiday was beginning to flag. One morning, several of us found sodden fragments of cement bags with 'Rugby Portland Cement' printed on them floating at low tide in shallow pools near the end of the pier. We idly wondered where they had come

Monitors on the school trip to Sandown, Isle of Wight.

from, told one or two of the teachers and, in no time at all, Cyril Bull seized his chance. After our midday meal he explained to the party what had been found, suggested various explanations, and offered a prize for the most convincing composition ('essays' came later). Some of us were sufficiently fired up to set to and write. We handed in our work the next day and eagerly waited for the winner to be announced. Typically, the head announced he had been quite unable to choose one from so many excellent compositions and said that every boy who had taken the trouble to write an account would receive a small cash prize. Of course, it came out of his pocket.

The staff also arranged coach trips to punctuate our fortnight. We visited Carisbrooke Castle, Shanklin Chine and Gadshill and enjoyed scrambling over the cliffs at Alum Bay to fill a glass tube with coloured sands to take home to our mothers. But the high spot of our stay one year was a visit to the local cinema, arranged at short notice when the weather turned nasty. *Top Hat* introduced me to the enduring delights of Fred Astaire and Ginger Rogers.

Because of Cyril Bull's connections and the reputation of the school, one of the perks of being in the top class was the opportunity to become a ball boy for the final Saturday of the Kent County Lawn Tennis Championships. These were held at the Rectory Fields, Blackheath, which was also one of the county cricket grounds. Mr Williams picked out a group of us who were good at drill and cricket; we were then given a special little homily by the head about our role, turnout, punctuality, good name of the school, etc. We had to find our own way over to Blackheath and back by public transport. On arrival at the ground, we were given brief instructions by one of the committee followed by a short rehearsal. Eventually, we found ourselves filing on to the court to crouch by the net or stand at the back. If it did not have quite the pomp and atmosphere of Wimbledon, we were sure it was the next best thing. There was a pleasant, blazered atmosphere, the sun beat down and we were regaled with lemonade at intervals. At lunchtime we ate our sandwiches lying on the grass in the shade of the trees and then played ball until it was time to restart. At the end of a long, hot day we were publicly thanked by our friend from the committee and presented with a box of used Dunlop balls each. We wanted no more and went home happy. As you will see, tennis balls were important to us.

NINE

BALLS & WHEELS

'To many of my generation, cricket has been a way of life, a gentle, humble, almost spiritual thing that aroused us and entertained us and captured so faithfully the spirit of a genteel age. It was grace and splendour; it inspired, almost demanded, attitudes of courtesy and camaraderie that set it apart from almost any other pursuit of life.'

The Game is not the Same, Alan McGilvray

Outside our house in Frederick Place, on the edge of the pavement, was a gas lamppost, the type with a horizontal bar below the glass lantern against which the maintenance man rested his ladder. The gas lamps were lit by the lamplighter, who arrived on his bicycle carrying a long rod with a hook on the end. He engaged this in one of the rings, which dangled below the lantern. A slow, steady tug and the gas lamp spluttered, coughed, and then burst into a soft yellow light.

It was against the base of this lamppost that I developed my cricket. The base was an ideal height and width for a wicket and as long as you hit the ball within a narrow arc there were few problems. At all costs, you had to avoid smashing windows in the houses nearby. It was not always possible to prevent the ball going into the narrow front gardens or down into an 'airey', but windows were the social danger. As I grew older and roamed further afield, our cricket shifted to Plumstead Common where we played with a hard ball and had plenty of room. But two or three of us still had occasional bouts of cricket against the lamppost right up to the outbreak of war.

I did not see much county cricket as a boy, although I loved the game this side of idolatry. I did not visit Lord's before the war but I did go to the Oval once or twice. I saw the ebullient Constantine and the West Indians in 1939 and I also saw Verity there. Like my friends, I was a keen autograph hunter and at the end of the day we lay in wait for the teams behind the stand. Several members of the Yorkshire side came out together, were disinclined to sign for us and made their way out of the ground to the

Plumstead Common.

Underground station. Professional cricketers, even Test cricketers, did not have private cars or arrive by taxi in those days; they travelled by public transport. We followed our heroes into the Underground and into the train and eventually captured the signature of Hedley Verity, the great England slow left-arm bowler. Many sportsmen were to die in the war but there were few deaths so keenly felt as that of Captain Verity, who died of his wounds in Italy in 1943.

My nearest county ground was Blackheath and the major cricketing event of the season was the match between Kent and Surrey there. Test matches were relatively few in the 1930s, so my interest was centred on the County Championship. Loyalties were fierce and enduring. I used to go there every year with two or three friends, equipped with sandwiches, an apple or banana, bottles of water, cricket bat and tennis ball, and settle down for the day by the boundary rope. During the lunch interval (we had long ago eaten our sandwiches) we moved on to the outfield to play cricket or French cricket, trying hard not to slog the ball into the crowd eating their lunch. The outfield was full of groups like ours and even a number of fathers were persuaded into action.

My parents with me as a young cricketer.

Although not so powerful as all-conquering Yorkshire, Kent and Surrey both had strong teams in the 1930s, with settled sides and solid opening partnerships. The names of Fagg and Todd and Fishlock and Gregory ring out across the years like those of old-established solicitors or estate agents. My most abiding memory of the matches I saw there is of Leslie Ames, Kent and England's great wicket-keeper batsman, delicately late-cutting with a short, chopping stroke or, beautifully balanced, flicking over-pitched balls off his toes and down to long leg.

The only other county ground I visited was Horsham, one of Sussex's prettiest grounds. We were staying at East Grinstead in 1938 and my father suddenly decided to have a day at the cricket and we set off to see Sussex play Derbyshire. Sussex were very much a band of brothers, with the Parks brothers, the Langridge brothers and the Oakes brothers, but possessed a limited pace attack. Derbyshire, on the other hand, were famous for producing fast bowlers and on that day they had the fiery-headed Copson and George Pope operating for them. I secured their autographs too, when they walked round from the pavilion to call in at the scorer's little tent. A summer day in the sun to cherish.

Besides cricket, we also played football in the road, again with a tennis ball, and 'catch', throwing the ball as high in the air as we could to each other. The main hazard here was the gullies in the gutters. To carry off the rainwater, the roads in our part of Woolwich had the usual cast-iron grids set in the gutters. In addition to these grids, presumably in case of violent storms, the side of the gutter next to the kerb was cut out into a rectangular hole, which led directly into the drain. These unlovely holes swallowed our tennis balls voraciously. It was a constant race to cut off balls thrown, struck or kicked too far or too inaccurately. Tennis balls were precious to us as they were the major ingredients in most of our games. Since they were relatively expensive, we sometimes reckoned our wealth on the number and quality of the balls we possessed.

Football was our game in the winter. I think I was about eight when I first became aware of, and interested in, professional soccer. Many people still associate Woolwich with the Arsenal football club. The club had originally been formed in the 1880s by an enthusiastic group of Arsenal workers and eventually became the first professional club in the south of England to join the Football League. However, as more London clubs joined, outside support fell away and local loyalty proved insufficient to keep the club in the town. So, in 1913, the Gunners, as they were called, moved to Highbury. After the First World War, the gap for football enthusiasts in the area was filled by Charlton Athletic, who played nearby at the Valley. It was this team, after its meteoric rise from the Third to the First Division in successive seasons, that I went to watch regularly with my father for several years.

Every other Saturday we had an early dinner and then set off for the Valley to arrive about 2.00 p.m. – kick-off was normally at 3.00 p.m. – so that I could get a place down by the railings close to the halfway line. Once across Academy Road, we joined the stream of spectators making their way along the Ha-Ha Road. We wound down Cemetery Road, round by Charlton Park, and into the vast stadium. A large wooden stand ran down one side and the only other covered accommodation lay behind one goal. Opposite the stand and behind the other goal an immense terrace rose skyward, so high that from the top the figures on the pitch looked like pieces on a green-baize board game. It seemed to me at the time an enormous stadium – and it was.

We had to wait almost an hour for the kick-off but I cannot recall being especially bored! Cold, yes, occasionally, but bored, no. There was the programme to read and discuss and then things livened up when the band (frequently the Royal Artillery band) marched out to entertain us. After they finished, excitement rose and it was only a minute or so before the familiar red-shirted figures trotted out of the tunnel to the strains of their signature tune, 'When the red, red robin comes bob, bob, bobbing along'. The club tried to get us to call them the Robins, but it never caught on. 'Addicks' they remained.

In the 1930s Charlton Athletic, like most teams, had a settled side free of constant injury, changes of management and boardroom wrangles. Their weekly wage approximated to that of a skilled craftsman. Several members of that promotion side spring easily to mind. There were the Oakes brothers, physically quite dissimilar, at the heart of the defence. John, large and powerful, played centre half while his squat, balding, gnome-like brother, Jimmy, was at left-back. Jimmy, perhaps because of his elderly appearance, was a favourite with the crowd. Harold Hobbis played outside left and because of his curiously lissom movements and sinuous running was aptly nicknamed 'Treacle'. He was one of a forward line that included regulars such as George Robinson, Lancelot, Tadman, Boulter and Wilkinson – no world-beaters there but good, honest professionals not given to dissent. If the best-known member of the Charlton side at that time was the wing half, Don Welsh, without doubt then the best-loved was the goalkeeper, Sam Bartram. Sam, with his mop of carroty hair and rakish cap, was renowned for his daring. He was always racing out from his line to throw himself at a forward's feet or to punch away a high centre. The next moment he would be flinging himself full-length from one side of his goal to the other. He made some inspirational saves but it was rather nerve-racking to watch at times. Knowledgeable supporters considered him the finest uncapped goalkeeper in the country though he was, perhaps, a little too daring for his own good and the selectors found his flamboyant style unnerving. At least the Valley never forgot Sam, and I was cheered recently to find that a close near the ground had been named in affectionate remembrance of him.

It was a different game in those days. The ball was made of leather and for much of the season it was wet and heavy, becoming more sodden and heavier as the pitch became muddier. It needed all a goalkeeper's power to reach the head of his centre-forward on the halfway line; it even required a substantial kick to curl in a deep centre. When the ball was heavy with mud it came down upon the head with something of the impact of a medicine ball, making an unforgettable squelchy smack upon the forehead. When little Jimmy Oakes took a high ball he seemed to shudder as the ball thudded onto his head, almost as though he was being driven into the pitch. The ball used to leave its imprint on his wrinkled forehead. Jimmy merely shook his head and grinned.

In those days the positions on the field appeared to be filled by men of quite distinctive build. Wingers were small, neat, tricky and very fast over the first few yards; inside-forwards were small, intelligent, calculating generals who linked defence and attack. The centre-forward, like his opponent, the stopper, was traditionally tall and powerfully built, dominant, a prince among players. Some physical licence seemed to be allowed to wing halves – for they were of two types: the first, tall, stylish, elegant; the second, squat, powerful and aggressive. Full-backs were always the same small, tough, tenacious, durable, nuggetty men, quick on the turn and rarely straying out of their own half.

During those few years before the war I must have seen all the famous First Division clubs but the team that remains most vividly in my memory is Arsenal. Arsenal, studded with internationals, was the great team of the 1930s and their match at the Valley was the high point of the season. Their visit, so keenly awaited, was the more interesting because of their origins in Woolwich. This, we felt, was the team we might have been privileged to cheer. When Arsenal came to Charlton, the ground was packed to capacity and crowds of between 65,000 and 70,000 were normal for this match of matches. There was a tremendous atmosphere and much of this tension and excitement revolved around the burly figure of the famous England centre-forward, Ted Drake. There was a roar of anticipation whenever the black-maned Drake, fast and powerful, moved on to the ball. Arsenal was a team of all-stars but despite Bastin, Compton, Hulme, Joy, Hapgood, Male and Copping, the man whom all schoolboys idolised, imitated and fantasised about was Drake.

In 1938 Arsenal recruited a small Welsh inside left called Bryn Jones from Wolverhampton Wanderers for the record transfer fee of £14,000. Although he never quite fulfilled his potential at Highbury (like so many contemporary sportsmen, his career was affected by the war) he scored the most memorable goal I ever saw. Jones received the ball some ten yards or so from the left touchline and it must have been all of forty-five yards from the goal. There was no other player near him. He checked, steadied himself, looked coolly at the goal and then quite deliberately struck a right-foot shot which rocketed into the top left-hand corner of the goal. Sam had been standing in the middle of his goal; he was still standing there when the ball hit the net behind him.

My parents and I at Eaglesfield.

Although Frederick Place was ideal for playing a variety of games, the road surface was unsuitable for roller-skating. Bloomfield Road, however, with a surface worn beautifully black and smooth by the buses, was ideal. When I first started roller-skating, metal skates with proper ball-bearing wheels and leather straps were expensive, costing 7s 6d a pair. You could adjust the length of the skates by using the special little spanner that came with them. They were made to last, and they did. Eventually the actual surface of the wheel would wear though leaving a rim, which produced a metallic rattling, and an uneven motion like a defective supermarket trolley. At first I was not allowed to skate down Bloomfield Road, so I started on the pavement above the Co-op. I trundled gently downhill and round the corner on to the forecourt trying to avoid old ladies with their shopping bags. Arms waving wildly to keep my balance, I came to an unsteady halt by turning my feet inwards. In due course I moved from the nursery slopes to the piste proper. Skating down Bloomfield Road was an exhilarating experience and we spent many happy hours in dry weather careering downhill, but I never became a first-class skater. I was not afraid of going fast but I was inhibited by my inability to stop quickly. I never mastered the technique of braking by placing the right foot at right angles behind the left and pulling up sharply with a shriek of wheels.

We also went on our skates up to Plumstead Common to a knoll near the bandstand. Here the winding, sloping, asphalted paths made a change from roads and pavements. At one point, by a memorial to the 8th London Howitzer Brigade, RFA TF, 1914–18, a steep serpentine path wound down between railings to a broad grassy hollow below. By some asphalting freak, this path had acquired distinctive markings revealing a sinuous black spine with dark-grey ribs springing from it on both sides. We called it Fishbone Alley and it was the acid test for roller skaters. The descent was rapid, the bends difficult to negotiate, and stopping at the bottom almost impossible. Only the most expert could manage it. The rest of us finished up clinging desperately to the railings or by being shot out at the bottom into a heap on the grass.

Bloomfield Road was also ideal for another of our activities which now seems to have disappeared, and that is 'carts' or what we called 'barrows'. Despite our irregular crazes and spasmodic fashions, at no time were my friends and I without our barrows. Basically, this was a short plank of wood fitted with an axle and a pair of pram wheels at each end. Ideally the rear wheels were larger than the front wheels but this was a counsel of perfection. To one end of the plank a strong wooden box, cut away to make a rudimentary seat, was nailed or screwed. The front axle was secured to a bar of wood upon which you rested your feet. Ropes, usually pieces of washing line, ran from each end of this front bar and you steered partly with these and partly with your feet. More sophisticated barrows had a wooden handbrake fixed to the side of the box acting on the rear wheel.

We made these barrows ourselves, borrowing the tools we needed from our fathers without their knowledge. Sometimes we needed help with the drilling and especially with the fixing of the front axle, so it was an advantage to have a father who was a fitter or a craftsman, or knew somebody who was. Pram wheels were not easily come by in my experience and assumed an importance even greater than that of tennis balls. We took pride in our barrows; many were well constructed and strong – they were not simply old boxes nailed onto rough old timber. Some had padded seats, while others had small boxes fixed behind the seat to carry tools, balls and boyish oddments. We vied with each other in speed and manoeuvrability, rattling two abreast down the hills and round the corners.

We played with our barrows round the block and on the two long hills of Bloomfield and Burrage Roads, but we did not go too far downhill because of the fag of having to haul them back uphill again. Occasionally, we used to take them over to the bandstand on Plumstead Common because this area was as good for barrows as it was for skating. We raced round the bandstand and rumbled down Fishbone Alley, bumping out on to the grass at the bottom until we trundled to a halt. Looking back, few things gave me as much pleasure as my barrow.

One of my friends about this time was a boy called Derek Sargent. He had a barrow-de-luxe and we played out together a great deal. He was about my size, equally thin, and possessed of an unearthly pallor. He lived above a shop, in the small wedge-shaped building in Conduit Road opposite the Baptist chapel. It was Derek who initiated me into the mystery of sex; you will have noticed that no mention of it has so far darkened my pages. One afternoon after school we were sitting on the front step of no. 88, talking idly about barrows when I became aware that Derek was dying to tell me something. Suddenly he whispered, 'Do you know what "f***" means?' I was aghast! I do not think I had ever heard one of my friends use that shocking, penalty-inviting, taboo word. I said that I did not. Using the broad-brush technique, Derek explained what it meant. I got the impression that he himself had only just been enlightened and was none too certain about some of the curious details. To my amazement he linked it with the process of producing babies.

Although there were occasions when we had casually wondered about the arrival of babies and the means of delivery, it was only a fleeting, not an all-absorbing, interest. Slightly older boys among us produced wild theories about how babies were created, where and how they grew. But when taxed with the vital question, they were equally confused about where the baby actually appeared from. We thought vaguely that it had something to do with our belly buttons but at that point speculation petered out – in any case, wasn't it time we had a game of football?

Derek put me right about this, too, but it seemed to me such an outlandish and bizarre process that I only half-believed him. Even so, he had opened a window on to what was to become an increasingly complex and disturbing world. But we did not immediately become obsessed with sex; we were certainly not equipped physically at that time for any kind of experiment. Nor was I or anyone I knew approached by unsavoury men in dirty raincoats or by acne-ridden older boys eager for experiment. There was no sex education at school; it was essentially a behind-the-bikesheds matter or a topic for the toilets. And, like most parents, mine were happy to steer clear of the whole subject. Besides, I had so many other important things to do and think about.

TEN

PARKS & COMMONS

'It was a saying of Lord Chatham, that the parks were the
lungs of London.'

William Windham, in a speech in the House of Commons
on 30 June 1808

Although the streets initially provided a useful playground for us, as
my friends and I grew older and bolder we looked for places where
we could play games of all kinds on a larger scale. Parks and
commons began to play a significant part in my life. These were the
venues where we played cricket in summer and football in winter, where
we climbed trees, made secret camps, acted out dramas from the Far West
and played 'Release'. Here, according to season, we picked blackberries
and pinched holly.

Of the three commons near my home, Winn's, Woolwich and
Plumstead, the first two may be briefly dismissed. Winn's Common was a
flat expanse on the western edge of my territory, which had a surface
devoid of grass and covered in small stones. It was a surface so
unattractive and so unsuitable, even for football, that we never used it. As
for Woolwich Common, when I lived in Herbert Road I was too young to
go and play there. Later on, when I became a cub, the pack did use the
common on occasions for tracking and other exercises but its very
openness, its lack of bushes and undergrowth, limited its appeal.

It was on Plumstead Common, three-quarters-of-a-mile long and
irregular in width, where I played most; so much variety in so little space!
A popular part of the common for us was the stretch opposite St
Margaret's Terrace, where the trunks of a line of plane trees made
excellent wickets. This was when there were only two or three boys
available; more serious games, of course, were played with stumps on the
main common. From the trees the ground sloped upwards to the top of
Fishbone Alley and to the bandstand where local bands gave concerts on
summer evenings. With my parents I often walked up there to join the

crowds sitting on the terraces at the back of the Globe Cinema overlooking the bandstand or simply strolling about listening to the music. This is one of my enduring memories. There was a magic about those pre-war summer evenings in the suburbs, a certain vibrancy, an electrical quality almost, in the air, a distillation of the faint noise of distant traffic and the indistinguishable cries and sounds from the tennis courts and common. A light summer dust seemed to pulsate in the warm air. As the twilight deepened, warmth rose from the asphalt and the pavements and the loom from unseen streetlights began to glow in the summer sky. I can still close my eyes and induce that special sensation.

Past the bandstand and across Blendon Road lay the main part of the common. The path began to rise with, on the left, a triangular area, with a surface only slightly better than that of Winn's Common. This is where we played our pick-up football games on Saturdays in winter, using our jackets for goalposts. There were, of course, no touchlines, only imaginary lines projected at imaginary right angles to a line through the jackets. This produced an elastic, lacrosse-like feeling about our boundaries and it was far easier to claim corners or goal kicks than throw-ins.

At the top of the slope the ground flattened out to reveal immaculately kept bowling greens and a trim little pavilion. Opposite were the tennis courts, hard and grass, although in those days I was more concerned in 'acquiring' tennis balls than actually playing. Further on, across another road, was the cricket ground proper, where many local clubs that did not have their own grounds played their matches – even Fox Hill played its matches there. This tended to be the climax of our family walks. We might listen to the band for a while but we were inexorably drawn across the common to the cricket. There were games on Saturday or Sunday afternoons stretching into the long summer evenings and clubs played evening matches during the week. Across the road from the pavilion stood two pubs, the Old Mill and the Prince Albert, both with forecourts filled with customers on warm nights, especially if an important match was being played.

Summer memories are full of this area. As I grew older I often went up there with a friend to sit and watch – and play about. The ground was separated from the road by a fence of concrete posts and horizontal steel rails, rails which were polished to a blue-black sheen by the hands and stomachs of the small boys who swung and revolved upon them. In my mind's eye, I can see the scuffed, tired strip of grass between the railings and the outfield where people sat or strolled to watch the game; the bare patches and dusty brown grass starred with fragments of silver paper, old bus tickets and little pieces of orange peel.

I enjoyed going up there with my parents because there was always the chance I might be treated to a cornet full of yellow ice cream from the

Italian vendor whose gaily striped cart with its bright brass covers was usually parked on the road nearby. My father always referred to him as 'old icy-creamo' or 'the hokey-pokey man'. I might add at this point that my father and his relatives and friends talked naturally about people of different races, colours or appearance, using expressions that have been outlawed for some years. But in those uncomplicated days, all foreigners were referred to in a jocular way. It was quite normal and there was no special malice or racist element in their comments. Several of the nicknames sprung from their war service overseas. Incidentally, I can hardly recall ever seeing a black man in Woolwich before the war, when they would have been regarded curiously as exotic creatures from another world. Which, indeed, they were. There were occasionally gypsy women who would call at the door, with babies swinging on their hips, selling lucky heather and clothes pegs. There was no serious anti-Semitism in our part of London as far as I was aware.

We bought ice cream only in the warm weather because we regarded it as a strictly summer delight. Normally ours came from the Walls ice-cream salesman (the 'Walleye man') who pedalled his tricycle around the London streets with the message 'stop me and buy one' painted on his container. Wafers and choc-ices cost 2*d* and cornets a penny. An early version of the iced lolly was just beginning to appear but from the marketing point of view the industry was still in its infancy.

My distant cousin, Eric, was often up there. He was a tremendously keen cricketer whose enthusiasm, like that of so many of us, sadly outstripped his talent. He batted well down the order, rarely stayed long enough at the crease to trouble the scorer, and was not often asked to bowl. Yet his passion for the game, his willingness to umpire, to score, to field as a substitute, act as twelfth man or make up the team at the shortest possible notice, ensured that he found a place of some kind in his side. When he was not actually playing himself at the weekends, he would travel all over the south-east by train and Green Line coach to watch county cricket or perhaps arrange to have a day with his Uncle Stan watching Essex. This made a change from his love-hate relationship with the players of his own county, Kent, whose failings, which he predicted in terms of 'you just wait and see', irritated him beyond measure. When you met him, even before you had a chance to ask him how he was, he would launch into a tirade, *à haute voix*, on the iniquity of the moment. When words finally failed him, red in the face, he would explode with his favourite adjective, 'useless!' Eric had no sense of humour – an essential quality for any cricketer.

Our own cricket was played on the stretch of grass opposite, bordering Plumstead Common Road. On fine evenings and Saturdays a line of games similar to ours stretched right along the common. It was always single-wicket stuff and, as there were so few of us, we could not afford much in the way of fielders, sometimes even dispensing with a wicketkeeper. Our games were played with a hard ball, not a pukka leather cricket ball (these were far too dear), but a 'compo' or composition ball. We did not have any pads and since we did not run to wicketkeeping gloves either, whoever was behind the stumps when one of our faster bowlers was operating used a jacket, preferably somebody else's, to trap the ball.

Everyone tried to bowl as fast as possible, pretending to be Larwood or Gover. We took very long runs and tended to decelerate as we reached the wicket. The fastest bowler among us was Freddie Smith, a chirpy, lively boy, about my own size, with an infectious grin and enormous stamina, who for a couple of seasons was my closest cricketing friend at Fox Hill. He would scud up and down, up and down, endlessly launching himself at the wicket from a run that started in the distance by the pavement railings. I quite fancied myself as a wicketkeeper batsman at that time (the Ames syndrome!) but one evening the dream was shattered. I was keeping wicket close behind the stumps to a quite innocuous bowler when the batsman, attempting to cut, got a top edge and the ball struck me just above the eye. I was dazed but not damaged, though I had a beautiful black eye for a week. I quickly decided to turn myself into an acrobatic cover point instead.

On those long summer evenings we would bowl our hearts out and bat and field for hours until the sun dipped behind the trees, the light faded, and it became hard to pick out the ball against the dark façades and brightly lit windows of the houses opposite. Then, with our stumps and bats under our arms, hot and tired, we would wander slowly home through the dusk looking for tennis balls.

Of the two parks of my boyhood, Eaglesfield and Shrewsbury, the latter was by far the more important. Eaglesfield (it was always known simply as that) stood on the crest of Shooter's Hill and really was a little too far away – and further uphill into the bargain. Its main attraction was a shallow round pond. When we were living in Herbert Road, my mother occasionally took me up there to sail my model yacht on it. What else do you do with a shallow pond? I was never really interested in model yachts; mine refused to sail properly and I became irritated waiting for the breeze to waft it back from the middle of the pond where it always seemed to get becalmed. The park itself sloped steeply, had no shrubbery and few trees. Admittedly there was a splendid view out across the golf course over the sprawling suburbs of north Kent and beyond, but since no part of the park was remotely suitable for football or cricket, its appeal was limited. I rarely visited it after we moved away to Frederick Place.

Shrewsbury Park (always pronounced 'Shroosbury') was a horse of a different colour. I mentioned earlier that this park was situated at the top of Plum Lane, just above my infant school. True, we did not choose to play football or cricket there (we preferred the shorter, flatter walk to Plumstead Common) but what it did offer were two distinct areas for some of our other activities. One part of the park was covered in thick undergrowth, mainly gorse and blackberry bushes and studded with birch, oak and chestnut trees. We burrowed into the undergrowth, careful to cover our trail and made secret camps known only to a few trusted braves. This was Indian country and from our hideaways we would creep out to attack wagon trains, passing cowboys and even other Indians. It was also ideal for playing our versions of such favourite games as release, prisoner's base and hide and seek. At one point the park sloped down to a hollow in which stood an old, gnarled hawthorn tree created by nature for climbing. Its mesh of branches was polished and made slippery by the feet and bottoms of generations of boys. Beyond the hollow was a wood of tall conifers, quite bare of undergrowth; only fitful sunlight filtered through the tops of the trees and it was always cool, silent and faintly sinister. Through this virgin forest we flitted, hid and fired at each other from behind tree trunks for hours on end.

Another attraction of the park was the drinking fountain with its large, cold, iron cup, secured by a chain to the side of the bowl. This was most welcome to hot, thirsty boys in high summer for we had no money to buy soft drinks or ice cream at the wooden refreshment hut that stood opposite the entrance on a triangle of grass. There was also a telescope where, for a penny, you could examine London and the Thames from St Paul's to Dagenham.

Immediately below Shrewsbury Park, an unmade dirt road, known as Sandy Lane, ran parallel to it. At one point there was something of a plateau upon which stood a modest tennis club with a little pavilion and two grass courts. During the two summers before the war, when I was attending St Olave's Grammar School, this became a particular haunt of mine with my special crony, Ralph Bugg. We were still not interested in tennis, or at that stage in the jolly girls, all pink and panting, bounding about before us; we were there for the balls. Buggy and I sat at the bottom of a short, steep bank close to the stop-netting, which was secured to the edge of the court and protected on the inside by 6in-wooden boards. Occasionally, balls lodged between the boards and the netting and then we would try to ease the balls out under the bottom and into our pockets while play was in progress. At the end of a set the players usually collected the balls before they left the court. If, after some searching, they found only five instead of six, they would give us hard looks; we merely stared blankly back at them. Sometimes one, more aggressive than the others, would ask us outright if we had seen the missing ball; we shook our heads and smiled sympathetically. We were pretty safe. Even if they had tried to catch us, we were on the outside of the court and would have been small specks disappearing into the middle distance before they were through the gate.

ELEVEN

COLLECTABLES

'And sometimes for an hour or so,
I watched my leaden soldiers go,
With different uniforms and drills,
Among the bedclothes through the hills.'

The Land of Counterpane, Robert Louis Stevenson

All boys collect things and I was no exception. Over the years I collected lead soldiers, stamps and cigarette cards. I bought my soldiers from two shops, Woolworths in Hare Street and Logans, a high-class toy shop in New Road near Woolwich Arsenal station. If you had little money and only wanted single soldiers, then Woolworths was the place to go. The soldiers, infantry and cavalry were laid out neatly on flat counters, separated according to type and price by glass divisions. Although cheap and attractive, they were slightly inferior to the real thing sold by Logans. Before William Britain invented the hollow-cast lead soldier, toy soldiers were solid figures made in France and Germany, but by the 1930s Britain's was the largest manufacturer of soldiers in the world. I sometimes wish I could take my daughters, grandchildren and great-grandchildren back in time to the toy counters of a pre-war Woolworths where nothing cost over sixpence. How they would delight in the range and quality of the goods!

All Britain's soldiers sold by Logans were offered in boxed sets, properly displayed in the window. Beautifully modelled cavalry, Life Guards, Scots Greys and Bengal Lancers came in boxes of five and cost, I think, 2s 6d. Infantry came in boxes of eight, the set usually including an officer. By far the most popular seemed to be the guardsmen in their red tunics and busbies who were modelled in three firing positions, prone, kneeling and standing. Other regiments were available but I cannot remember seeing, let alone collecting, any khaki-clad figures; I seem to have been encapsulated in the late-nineteenth century. Perhaps the most attractive box of all was that containing a complete guards' band. I was lucky enough to have one of these and I treasured it and kept it in pristine condition for years. Also in the window were field guns of various calibres and several spectacular items such as horse-drawn guns and limbers, horse-drawn ambulances and searchlight units, all of which cost more than I could afford.

Logans sold model steam engines and Hornby 0-gauge trains and also the 00 gauge when these appeared in the late 1930s. I had a modest clockwork train set with passenger coaches and goods wagons but my layout was necessarily limited (we only had small rooms). Despite my train-spotting activities, I never became a railway buff, though I must admit I was sorely tempted when I pressed my nose against the window to drink in the details of the goods wagons, signal gantries, tunnels and model stations complete with miniaturised platform equipment. Logans also sold air pistols, cricket bats, roller skates and fishing rods so you can appreciate what an Aladdin's cave it was. Ah, my Hornby and my Britain long ago!

My father made me a fine fort, with a square-battlemented tower, and I used to spend long hours planning and fighting imaginary battles. In the summer, I could move my troops out on to more realistic terrain in the garden, concealing my men in rough trenches along the edge of the flowerbeds, while the supporting cavalry lurked in reserve behind a forest of stocks. My small army grew steadily and gave me much pleasure. I was still playing with them occasionally, though I hope in a more sophisticated way, when I was sixteen.

Stamp collecting was a winter hobby. I suppose I collected off and on from the age of six until I left school, but it was many, many years before I could bring myself to dispose of my stamps. I started off with a cheap album with thin leatherette covers, which cost a shilling. On each page was printed the name of the country and beneath it certain salient facts including capital city, population, area in square miles and major products. At this stage I collected everything and anything. Although I had no relatives working in banks (a rich source of supply) or travelling abroad, both my Uncle George and my Uncle Charles had small collections, which they passed on to me. I spent hours laboriously removing and cleaning their stamps and mounting them proudly in my new album. Large packets of assorted foreign stamps were cheap and they helped to flesh out one's album. My friends and I were particularly attracted by the cheap and cheerful French colonial issues and by the more expensive and elegant stamps of the British colonies; best of all in our eyes, however, were the delightful stamps of Haile Selassie's Abyssinia. Packets of stamps of various kinds, special offers, unbeatable and unrepeatable bargains, were all advertised in the comics and magazines we read, and stamps frequently featured as free gifts in promotional schemes to boost their sales.

As with most boyhood hobbies, our interest waxed and waned. When stamps suddenly became all the rage we would go to school armed with tweezers, perforation gauge and magnifying glass, plus a wallet in which we stored our duplicates for swapping. It was all very harmless, as long as you did not get carried away by the approval system. Stamp dealers advertised in our magazines offering books of stamps of various categories on approval. No money in advance was required; you merely sent away for what you were interested in. The stamps arrived in booklets looking rather like a modern chequebook, neatly mounted and individually priced. The booklets we sent for were in the 2s 6d to 5s class and you had to return the money or the stamps within a certain time. Usually we took what we wanted and then hawked the booklets round among our friends and at school. Most of the stamps we bought were priced at a farthing or a halfpenny; we would occasionally splash out a penny but we rarely went higher.

We could not afford to buy copies of *Stanley Gibbon's Stamp Catalogue* but we could consult it at the junior library in Woolwich. We used to pore over its pages to see how much our 'best' stamps were worth, though I am afraid few of them were in a condition to appeal to a dealer or a serious collector. I absorbed much from my stamps over the years. As well as the geographical locations, I picked up a knowledge of the world's currencies, details of kings, queens, and presidents, and a surprising amount of information from pictorial issues, especially those from France, America and our own British colonies.

Stamp collecting is alive and well; cigarette cards, sadly, were another casualty of the war, though the sets are much in demand by collectors today. Between the wars the major cigarette companies, Players, Wills, Rothmans, Carreras and Gallaghers, all included cards in their packets of ten and twenty. The cards were based on popular themes ranging from film stars to fish, from cricketers and footballers to cars and birds. They usually came in sets of fifty and you could stick them in special albums, either as you went along or when you had a complete set. I said, 'could' but, in fact, my friends and I did not. We used to keep our various sets secured by elastic bands in shoeboxes; I had a second shoebox in which I kept all my spares, and that was full, too.

You may wonder how we managed, as non-smokers, to collect so many cards. Our main source of supply was our parents, relations and friends; the latter, knowing of our interest, would save their cards and pass them on to us when we met. The secondary source was one which, in retrospect, makes me go hot and cold. We simply used to stop men in the street with the time-honoured cry, 'Got any fag cards, mister?' Usually I went out and did this with a friend but sometimes I did it alone. We used to accost men at random on our way to and from school or while we were playing out in the evenings. We would also waylay men returning from work or on their way back from watching the cricket on summer evenings. Certain points on Plumstead Common and the junction of Plumstead Common Road with Burrage Road were particularly profitable pitches. Fortunately, none of us ever came to any harm – but then you rarely, if ever, did in the 1930s.

Another source, although not generating quite the sheer volume of cards as the other two, was the most interesting. When collecting cards was suddenly the craze at Fox Hill, we used to play 'fag cards' in the playground at break and at dinnertime when the weather was fine. The card players who gathered along the wall by the lavatories were of two types – pitch-holders and players. The pitch-holder would squat down close to the wall and arrange his options. He could lean a card vertically against the wall, fold a card in two and place it a few inches in front of the wall, or he could bend the edges of the folded card back about a quarter of an inch so that it looked rather like a witch's hat. So you had a row of pitch-holders, offering cards in a variety of positions, and encouraging the players to patronise them by shouting the odds. The players knelt or crouched down several feet from the wall (our oche was a standardised distance pragmatically arrived at and rigidly enforced) and attempted to flick a card with their index and middle fingers to knock the pitch-holder's card over. If successful, the player was rewarded roughly along the following lines. It was fairly easy to knock over a card leaning against the wall and for that he received one card plus his own card back. It was not quite so easy to knock over the folded card so he got two cards for this. Turning the carefully folded and bent card upside down demanded accurate and forceful play and he won four cards for this. All cards that missed were gathered in and kept by the pitch-holder.

It was a busy corner with small boys clutching packs of fag cards in their hands moving from pitch to pitch according to slight variations in the odds. Those who were skilled in the accurate flicking of fag cards tended to remain players. I can still do this today; it is like riding a bicycle, a skill once acquired that never deserts you. Less successful players would seek to recoup their losses by becoming pitch-holders.

One entrepreneurial development of our play was the employment of the most-skilled flickers by boys who had little skill themselves but had a store of cards and ambitions for a larger one. It so happened that my friend, Fireplace, had magic in his fingers and I employed him from time to time when I was going through a lean spell, having first agreed on his fee of so many cards of his choice. Obviously, the stiffer the card, the better and more effective it was to flick and Fireplace was expert on the playing merits of cards from the various companies. He used to make quite a useful profit for me.

While we are at Fox Hill, I can deal briefly with the other games we played there. Several traditional games for boys were on the wane in the mid-1930s in my part of London. Boys bowling hoops, for example, were something of a rarity. Their hoops were made of metal and were propelled by a short metal rod with a hook at the end to grip the hoop. I remember my parents telling me that in their childhood, in the early years of the century, there were definite seasons for playing certain games such as bowling hoops, marbles and whipping tops, but this was no longer so in the 1930s.

We did still play marbles, though it was a simplified, lacklustre version of the game my father played. There was nothing in it of the circle and shooting an alley with your thumb to knock your opponent's marbles out of the ring. We played a version in the playground where two players rolled their marbles alternately; we used glass ones although there were still earthenware ones about. If you struck your opponent's marble, you took it; if you missed you had to let your marble remain where it was while your opponent tried to strike it. And so it went on until the bell rang, or one of you lost his little stock of marbles, or you became bored.

We also played a linear version of marbles along the gutters on the way home from school. The same rules applied but we tended to lose marbles down the gullies, although this did not matter too much since marbles were not valuable like tennis balls. I also remember playing spasmodically with a whip and a top, but this was a very minor pursuit and was mainly played by the little boys at the bottom end of the school.

For us, such pastimes were not so much seasonal as the manifestation of sudden crazes and fashions. One day someone would produce a bag of marbles and the game would run through the school like wildfire and continue for a week or so until it died as suddenly as it arose, to be replaced by some new phenomenon. The late 1920s and '30s were a time for crazes of all kinds. There was diabolo (my mother was naturally very adept at this, my father and I were hopeless) and the more enduring yo-yo. Who remembers the arrival of the biffbat, which cost 6d and consisted of a small rubber ball attached by a length of elastic to the centre of a table tennis bat?

There was one seasonal game, however, which is still going strong – conkers. In the autumn we made our way to the common to throw lumps of wood up into the horse chestnut trees to knock the precious conkers down. There are few more pleasing experiences than splitting open a spiky green husk to reveal the bright mahogany jewel nestling within. We bored a hole in them with a metal skewer, passed a piece of stout string through and tied a double knot at the end. I need only comment here that it was often the wrinkled, battered conker that smashed its opponents to smithereens and not the glossy produce fresh from the husk. Some boys thought a conker's performance could be improved by baking it in the oven or soaking it overnight in vinegar, but I never bothered with this. All these games virtually stopped for me when I left Fox Hill and started to travel up by train to my London grammar school in Tooley Street near Tower Bridge.

This move also meant that my pocket money was increased from 1*d* to 2*d* a week. You may consider my basic rate absurdly small; I can only say that I may not have had much but my friends, with one exception, did not seem to have more. I cannot remember ever being without a copper or two in my pocket and, of course, the purchasing power of pennies then was considerable.

During my years at Fox Hill, I enjoyed a penny a week, which I spent on sweets. Almost all varieties of ordinary sweets were 2oz for a penny, so you received quite a useful little bag for a halfpenny. I tended to buy two halfpenny bags of different sweets each week, though occasionally I would be seduced into buying from a range of cheap specialities priced at a farthing: gobstoppers, liquorice sticks, and sherbet dips. I bought my sweets at Sergeant's round the corner in Bloomfield Road. Although the shop had the name Sergeant on the front, it was actually run by a kindly but slightly mysterious, stout, bald-headed man with gold-rimmed spectacles whom we called Mr Butchard. Some people said he was originally a German, and he did have a curious accent, but I never discovered anything about his past and his little shop did not survive the war. On the rare occasion when I was particularly flush, I spent a whole penny on my favourite, 'Palm toffee'. This came in a slab and the Pickwickian Mr Butchard used to crack it into small pieces with a special hammer he kept underneath the counter and let the lumps drop into the brass pan on his scales.

At this time the standard 2oz bar of chocolate cost 2*d* and was way beyond the means of those of us who now travelled up daily to school from Woolwich Arsenal to London Bridge, except Gerald Plaistow. Gerald came from a superior home and had more pocket money than any of us, although, to be fair, he was always generous and invariably broke off a square of chocolate for each of us. Just before the war, a new bar of chocolate was introduced called the 'Double Six' – I cannot remember the name of the manufacturer – which had more, slightly smaller, sections than the other bars and was very popular with us. Its success was short-lived for, like so many of my boyhood delights, it vanished with the coming of the war, which swept sweets and chocolates from the shelves.

This talk of a penny a week for pocket money is misleading. As I grew older my father, who was paid monthly, started giving me what he called 'the odd'. At the end of the month he would go to the bank, usually on a Saturday morning, and after dinner when the dishes were cleared and the tablecloth removed, he would turn out the notes and coins on to the table while I knelt up excitedly in my chair to watch the proceedings. First, he would give my mother her housekeeping. My mother was a competent manager and she paid all the domestic expenses from her housekeeping money. I think the only thing my father had to deal with was the monthly mortgage cheque to the building society, but because of his reluctance to settle down and do this or, indeed, to write letters of any kind, my mother had to nag away at him for days on end, a monthly ritual which exasperated her. Next he would take his own modest pocket money and then (the great moment!) pass over to me the odd coppers or even the sixpence that were left. I can see his hand now moving the coins across the green chenille cloth towards me. One curious thing that struck me about my father was that he always appeared to have a pocketful of loose change, something I never achieved in adult life.

Even so, you may wonder how I managed to finance my collecting of stamps, soldiers and other items. My small working capital was derived partly from 'the odd' but mainly from postal orders I received from relatives at Christmas and for my birthday. Again, friends and relatives rarely visited us, or we them, without pressing a sixpence or sometimes even a shilling into my eager, little palm – one of the benefits of being an only child! All this money I saved up carefully. My friends and I all had Post Office savings books and into mine went most of the monies I received. Parents and relations stressed the need for saving against a doubtful tomorrow so the habit was inculcated into me from an early age. I began to recognise the value of money, a respect for its attainment and a care in its spending that conditioned me for life.

TWELVE

SEA & SAND

'I do like to be beside the seaside,
I do like to be beside the sea.
I do like to stroll along the prom, prom, prom
Where the brass band plays pom tiddly om pom pom!'
                'I Do Like to Be Beside the Seaside', J.A. Glover-Kind

If a madeleine aroused Proust's memories of his childhood, for me recollections of our seaside holidays are stirred by the image of the cabin trunk. This trunk, brown in colour and banded in wood, was kept under my parent's bed. About a fortnight before our holiday, my mother pulled it out, lifted the lid, and removed the tray. From the inside

Having a paddle with Mother.

Above: On the merry-go-round.

Right: On the beach with my cousin Roy and the dog.

emanated a slightly musty smell, a breath, faint but unmistakeable, of the seaside. No matter how carefully she had cleaned it out the previous summer, there was always a dusting of sand in the bottom: sand from Bognor or sand from Southsea, sand from Ilfracombe or St Leonards-on-Sea. These were the resorts where, like our relatives and friends, we spent two weeks by the sea in August.

I used to enjoy helping my mother pack the trunk. Out from various drawers and cupboards appeared swimming costumes, rubber beach shoes, sun hats and holiday items I had not seen for a whole year. We did not have any special holiday wear; we simply wore our normal summer clothes. All we needed for that wonderful fortnight by the sea had to be carefully thought out, washed, ironed and packed, and then the trunk was locked and sent off a week in advance by rail to our boarding house.

Once the trunk was ready, my parents carried it downstairs and stood it on end in the hall and my father put the 'card' in the front downstairs window. This card, about six inches by eight, had the letters 'CP' (which stood for Carter Paterson, the major London carrier) boldly printed in red on a green background. Their vans used to cruise the district and wherever the driver spotted a CP card in a window he would stop and call. He took his load of trunks, boxes, cases and goods of all descriptions to the station where they passed into the efficient hands of the Southern Railway to be sent all over England. I used to be impressed when we arrived at our seaside lodgings and found our familiar brown trunk standing invitingly in a corner of our bedroom.

On the beach with Mother and Father.

We travelled to the seaside by train, lightly laden, with me carrying my bucket and spade, not so much because buckets are difficult to pack (which they are) but because I wanted neighbours and friends to know where I was bound. The buckets and spades grew slowly larger as the years of childhood passed.

Where did we stay? Certainly not in hotels. We started by taking rooms and later on, when we were a little better off, we stayed in boarding houses. This taking of rooms was a curious arrangement, a staging post on the way to self-catering but without the kitchen. We had a bedroom, which I shared with my parents, and a sitting-cum-dining room. The landlady gave us breakfast but we operated an unusual victualling system for our supper. My mother used to bring in the food, some chops, steak or a 'bit of fish' (I cannot remember her buying vegetables, though I imagine she must have done) and the landlady would cook it for us.

Our seaside holidays were traditional ones, and essentially beach holidays. Given reasonable weather, we followed a certain routine. Every

Drinking with Father.

Off to the beach.

morning after breakfast we proceeded to the beach; sandy at Bognor, shingle at St Leonards-on-Sea, stony at Brighton. I often think that if only Brighton, the most exhilarating town west of Suez, had a sandy beach it would be hailed as the premier resort in Europe, a kind of Nordic Monte Carlo or cold-water Cannes, especially if it were only somewhat warmer and the prevailing south-west breeze slightly less bracing.

We set off with our beach towels, bathing costumes, stumps and cricket bat (depending on the tide and the nature of the beach), bucket and spade, and a large bag for our necessaries. Costumes for men and boys were one-piece affairs reaching down towards mid-thigh, often with coloured horizontal stripes across the chest. My father could not swim but he usually changed and came in to splash about with us. My mother was a strong swimmer with a slow, deliberate over-arm stroke but she had no success in her attempts to teach me to swim. And there we stayed with our deckchairs and our picnic, reading, dozing, paddling and swimming, building sandcastles with concentric walls which were never able to resist the incoming tide, and playing cricket, French cricket and catchball when the tide was out.

With Mother on the ferry to the Isle of Wight.

On the beach with mother.

There is little point in a beach as such unless you can play cricket on it, and this is where we score heavily over our friends around the Mediterranean. Their soft, golden sands are wholly unsuitable for serious pursuits. There is no batting surface to compare with that firm, gleaming, mud-coloured expense of recently exposed sand around the English coast. I huddled out of the wind behind a groyne, silently urging the laggard tide to back off and reveal its treasure. As the sea receded, first from the sloping shingle bank and then from that intermediate area of shingle and sand studded with large stones, to expose a thin strip of sand proper, small boys would suddenly appear from nowhere and leap and shout and cavort at the water's edge.

At this point, I encountered one of the snags of being an only child. As soon as a reasonable stretch of sand had been exposed and had partially dried out, families would descend and set up stumps and start the proper business of the morning. Although you can play a sort of cricket with three people, it is a little hard on the parents who do all the bowling and fielding. I used to look enviously at large families with their wealth of fielders and long to join them. Fathers and uncles would bowl slow over-arm stuff at their sons and daughters; sons would race across the sand and hurl the tennis ball in a flurry of arms and legs; mother, aunts and soppy girls would bowl under-arm but with guile. Girls could not bat for toffee, of course, but they all had to have a turn. High up on the stones, grandma looked up from her knitting from time to time and nodded approvingly. Slumped in a deck chair beside her slept grandad, dead to the world, barefoot, his chalk-white feet brilliant in the sunshine, his trousers rolled halfway up his shins, and a handkerchief with a knot tied at each corner protecting his head.

The solution to my problem was straightforward. My father would approach a father who appeared to be in charge of a sizeable game (at the end of an over, naturally) and ask if his son could join in. This favour was always granted and I scampered out to the deep, or rather to the edge of the deep, hoping to show off by taking a high catch or display my fleetness of foot by squelching through the shallows. These newfound friends were always punctilious in giving the new boy his turn and generous in their

At a gymkhana at Clacton in 1931. We three are on the front row on the right.

bowling. There are few things more satisfying than the solid smack of a wet tennis ball driven high over mid-wicket into the sea.

Working the beach were men selling kites, ice cream, newspapers, comics and magazines. I looked forward to buying a brightly coloured special packet, which cost sixpence – a lot of money to me; you could only buy these packets at the seaside and they, too, disappeared with the war. They contained an amazing assortment of things dear to a small boy's heart: games, puzzles, comics and things like whistles, compasses and dice.

Every morning we looked in the paper to see if Lobby Ludd was visiting our particular seaside town that day. Lobby Ludd was an inconspicuous but identifiable man who, during the summer, visited resorts along the South Coast. The dates of his visits, together with his photograph, were well publicised and he arranged to be near a prominent landmark in the town at a certain time. If you thought you spotted him, you confronted him, being careful to use the correct challenge, which went something like this, 'You are Lobby Ludd and I hereby claim my £5 prize.' Well, I think it was £5 but we never came across him or heard of anyone who had actually seen him and won a prize.

The highlight of our fortnight was the visit to a show towards the end of the second week. This usually meant the theatre at the end of the pier, the White Rock Pavilion at Hastings, or the Floral Hall at Bognor. We saw the Fol-de-Rols and Clarkson Rose's 'Twinkle' and I have a disturbing memory of Douglas Byng at Bognor doing a number called 'I'm Doris, the Goddess of Wind'. I could not see anything funny in it but my father nearly fell off his seat. My 'What's funny about that, Dad?' received no answer.

I should stress at this point how good my parents were in meeting my demands for various ball games, whether it was cricket in the backyard or on the beach, rounders in the park or catchball in any field. They bowled and threw and ran and caught without complaint until I was too tired to carry on. My mother was, in retrospect, rather surprising. As far as I could see, she was quite unlike the mothers of my friends. Although slender, she was vigorous physically and without being good at any particular sport, she was generally athletic. She could swim, she had a very good eye with a bat or a tennis racquet, she could throw a tennis ball hard and accurately under-arm and take a high catch or a swift return with ease. I know I was an only child but I marvel at their patience and kindness.

I am also indebted to my parents for an early introduction to castles, stately homes, gardens, cathedrals and museums. They were both genuinely interested in seeing 'old places' and our long days on the beach were usually punctuated with visits by service bus or special coach tours to places of interest. Thus I saw cathedrals at Canterbury, Chichester and

On the rocks with Father.

Winchester, castles at Hastings, Bodiam, Amberley, Corfe, and Arundel, the Cheddar Caves, and perhaps best of all, HMS *Victory* in Portsmouth Dockyard on Open Day. I found being conducted round this warship intensely exciting, and I remember how moved I was when we went below and stood, hushed, in the lamp-lit gloom where Nelson died.

Too soon came the moment for the trunk to be packed, re-labelled and despatched to London. There was time for one last, long day on the beach, one final swim, and then goodbye sea and sand until next year. A few days after we arrived home the Carter Paterson van would draw up outside the house and the driver would bring the trunk into the hall. My parents carried the trunk upstairs into their bedroom, and then I found a melancholy pleasure in helping my mother to unpack. These articles, which only a few short days ago had offered promise of delight, now seemed limp and devoid of life. We put a heap of soiled clothes on the floor to go downstairs; we shook the sand out of my beach shoes and my mother's swimming cap and set the bathing costumes on one side to be washed and carefully stored away. Together we slid the empty trunk under the bed until next year. I straightened up and realised that summer was a-dying.

THIRTEEN

JAUNTS & JOLLITIES

'The motor-car went poop-poop-poop, as it raced along the
road. Who was it steering it into a pond? Ingenious Mr Toad.'
The Wind in the Willows, Kenneth Graham

Throughout the Frederick Place years, my carefree humdrum existence was punctuated by visits and excursions. I have described our usual fortnight's holiday by the sea but there were also visits to relatives in London and Sussex and day excursions to places of interest in the summer. As my mother said, 'We always go somewhere on Bank Holiday, dear.'

Motorised jaunts revolved around my father's brother, George, whose family lived not far away in Eltham. We used to go and have tea with them at irregular intervals, walking to Academy Road to catch the tram, which went swaying and moaning down the hill from the police station at the bottom of Shooter's Hill, past the Welcome Inn and on to Well Hall. Uncle George, a lean and somewhat cadaverous soul with a pencil-thin black moustache, suffered under a squat and formidable wife called Floss. This was short, I imagine, for Florence; it could have hardly been a pet name since she appeared the antithesis of the light, sweet and agreeable. Uncle George's main source of pleasure was his car – a rarity in our circle – and sometimes he and Floss would drive over to Plumstead to take us out for a run. I loved this; my mother dreaded it. Uncle George had never taken any kind of driving test and he proceeded at a stately pace along the crown of the road. He never used any hand signals and paid little heed to other road users or their frustrated horn blowing. We did not go very far; we did not drive to the South Coast for the day or anything like that, not even as far as Sevenoaks or Tonbridge. Instead, on a summer's evening, we trundled southwards along the arterial roads in the direction of Bromley and Orpington. The high point of the run, as far as I was concerned, was the customary stop for refreshments at a large roadside pub on the way back. It never crossed Uncle George's mind to seek a country pub in one of the attractive villages a few miles off the main road – perhaps he was concerned about the width of the road. The four adults would go in for a drink, though my mother never 'drank' as such, only a soft drink, leaving me in the car. My father would bring me out a glass of ginger beer and a packet of cheese biscuits. This ritual never varied. In due course we would drive sedately home with Uncle George even more in the middle of the road than usual.

The only other relatives we had in London were my mother's sister, Dorothy (Dot) and her husband, Jack, who lived in a flat in Ashmore Road in Kilburn. We visited them from time to time, occasionally spending the night there. Uncle Jack was a well-spoken, smart-looking man, who worked as a waiter in a West End hotel, but waiters were poorly paid and there was little money to spare. The flat was plainly furnished, with linoleum on the floors, and was lit by gas. Their only son, my cousin Roy, was a couple of years old at this time and not really big enough for me to play with. After tea, his mother used to bath him in a small tin bath in front of the kitchen range, always using Wright's Coal Tar soap. Even today the pungent smell of Wright's Coal Tar soap, admirable soap though it may be, still makes me feel slightly queasy. Auntie Dot dried him, sat him on the edge of the kitchen table, and proceeded to clean his ears and nose vigorously with an orange stick and cotton wool. Roy did not like this and I did not enjoy watching it. Afterwards, he would be put down in his cot and I would sleep in a single bed by his side with the gaslight turned down low, hissing and popping in the quiet.

Our main days out, however, were to my father's home at East Grinstead and to my mother's at Brighton. As most of their brothers and sisters were still at home or living in the vicinity, it gave me a chance of seeing my aunts and uncles fairly often. To reach East Grinstead we took the tram to Victoria and then caught the Green Line coach. Put down in the High Street, we made straight for the house in Queen's Road. At first, when I was tiny, my grandparents were there to welcome us but after my grandmother's death my aunts, Bess and Nell, looked after the house and its occupants. We also went round the corner to West Street to call on 'Brother Jim' and his wife, Kit. There was an unofficial arrangement that we had dinner at Queen's Road with the aunties and tea with Kit and Jim, or vice versa; it helped to spread the load. As you may suppose, I was made a great fuss of by all of them but I liked Uncle Jim the best, probably because he was always willing to play with me. He certainly passed the child's infallible test for a grown-up with flying colours.

When I first became aware of him he was driving the local dustcart. Under his cap, his bucolic features (he was a different physical type from my father) had a dark-red hue and he wore a thick, collarless striped shirt, open at the neck. If we met him out while he was working, he greeted us with a great grin and a wave of his hairy arm from the cab. He never wore a collar or tie, even on Sundays, which was the day we often seemed to call on them. On these occasions, he wore a clean, striped shirt fastened with a gold stud, blue serge trousers held up (or 'prevented from falling down' as he used to say) by leather braces and a leather belt so wide it almost resembled a narrow corset.

Jim had a hearty appetite and he sat down for his usual Sunday dinner – roast beef and Yorkshire pudding with a small mountain of roast potatoes, surrounded by mounds of vegetables – with his knife and fork clutched purposefully in his big fists. He ate this with obvious relish, wiping his mouth with the back of his hand from time to time and looking forward to his heavy pudding. After dinner, he retired to a wooden armchair by the kitchen range, unlaced his boots, blew out his cheeks, and fell fast asleep. His sleep was punctuated by sudden stertorous spasms, which convulsed his upper body without waking him. Kit used to poke him hard on the shoulders to shut him up but it had no effect. He woke up about 4 p.m. with an innocent beaming smile and demanded his tea. This he poured into his saucer, blew on, and sucked noisily down.

In his bluff, awkward way, Jim was kind to me as a child. He and Kit had no children of their own (I never knew why) and I do not think he came into contact with them much. He was also a part-time member of the local fire brigade (he naturally drove the fire-engine) and at my urging he would get out his brass helmet and let me parade up and down in it. He also taught me to play 'up the line' with halfpennies. We stood about 6ft from the wall of his living room and lobbed halfpennies to see who could get nearest to the skirting board. Somehow or other I always just managed to pip him. Then suddenly, without warning, he would be racked by spasms of the most frightful coughing (he had been gassed in 1918) which left him crimson in the face and gasping for breath.

Jim's table manners and dress upset my mother for their lack of refinement. Years later, after the war, he occasionally came down to St Leonards-on-Sea for the day to visit them. My parents would meet Jim and Kit off the coach in town, and Jim would amble towards them, smiling broadly in his pre-1914 outfit of blue serge suit, cap, boots and striped shirt, with his gold stud glinting in the sun. He enjoyed a breath of sea air and a stroll along the promenade and was eager to be off. My mother suffered agonies of embarrassment accompanying him along the front and then choosing to have a cup of tea in some obscure little café, fearful of meeting any of her friends. She would have gladly settled for an afternoon on the lawn, screened from the neighbours, with a dainty tea nicely served.

In the afternoons at East Grinstead my father would take us out for a walk into the town or into the immediate countryside. He enjoyed visiting the scenes of his youth and telling us stories of his boyhood. Sometimes we simply crossed over onto the cricket ground to play ball, my father never failing to remind me how the mighty Bonnor, long ago, had smashed several windows in West Street with his hitting. More often in the spring and summer we would go for our favourite walk to Mill's Rocks. The three of us would walk up West Street, out past the charming old buildings in the High Street culminating in Sackville College and the Parish Church, and on to the Forest Row road. After a little way, we struck off left across the fields and down into the woods where in spring the trees seemed to rise from a mist of bluebells. Further on, we came to Mill's Rocks – one of several outcroppings in the area – and I would climb and scramble over them until I was worn out. Then, loaded with bluebells for my aunts, we would catch the bus from Ashurst Wood back to the town. If we were visiting East Grinstead for the day it meant a long journey home for me. I slept most of the time, slumped against the side of the coach, before being roused at Victoria to change onto the tram, and then shaken awake again at Woolwich to walk home.

My memories of Brighton are, of necessity, much more slender. The absence of a family house and the dispersal of Nana's children made our visits there of a different order. Brighton did not have the small country town, old-fashioned atmosphere of East Grinstead, nor did I experience the feeling of clannishness so palpable around Queen's Road. Brighton, being 'the seaside', had a raffish, attractive air about it; indeed, when I was first taken there, the air was so strong it made me unwell. Eventually, I grew acclimatised and I became aware of its many charms. We went down by train from Waterloo, usually for the day, but very occasionally to stay for the weekend or for a few days. Nana lived in a small terrace house in Whicheloe Place near Queen's Park and off the long hill that led up from the sea front to the racecourse. We spent most of our time on Brighton's pebbly beach and we travelled up and down from the promenade on the trams that ran up Queen's Road from St James' Street. On the lower deck you sat facing each other on long, perforated wooden seats that ran the length of the car. The upper deck was open and you sat on wooden seats with slatted backs, which could be reversed for the return journey. I always plunged upstairs to sit with the breeze blowing on my face while the tram slowly groaned its way up the steep hill.

Nana later moved round the corner to 17 Toronto Terrace, where she became housekeeper to a portly, white-haired moustached bachelor affectionately known to the family as 'Uncle Arthur'. Uncle Arthur Hall was a postman (I have his postman's clock) and appeared in all the wedding photographs of the time. Some years ago Dot told me that Nana had once confided to her that Uncle Arthur was always the perfect gentleman and had never attempted so much as to lay a finger on her.

Their small terrace house was brimming full with furniture. The front room, only used on high days and holidays, contained a sideboard, dining table and chairs, as well as a three-piece suite and a piano. Sometimes, my mother could be persuaded to play upon it and I remember her tapping away contentedly while aunts and uncles gathered round her. Better still, when the adults were out or busy elsewhere, I used to creep in and 'practise' on my own. The room was so small that when we crowded in for Sunday dinner or for tea, we all had to edge in through the door and slide in carefully between the edge of the table and our chair. And once you were in, you were in until the meal was over.

Our walks and non-beach activities tended to circle around Queen's Park, not far away down the hill. Occasionally, on non-race days we would walk even further up the hill to the windswept expanse of Brighton racecourse – a long walk for little legs. As I grew older I discovered the pleasures of the West and Palace piers. There had once been a famous Chain Pier, too, the first of the pleasure piers, constructed in 1823 and designed on the same principle as a suspension bridge. Built on four massive ironclad piers, it even had small shops built into its hollow towers. It became a prominent attraction of the town and featured in paintings by both Constable and Turner. Eventually, this splendid structure was swept away by a fierce storm in 1896. Nana's brother, Charlie, who lived round the corner, had made a superb model of this pier out of matchsticks and it stretched the length of his sideboard in a glass case. I have often wondered what became of this museum piece. The Palace Pier at the bottom of the Steine was my favourite because it possessed an exciting range of machines in its amusement hall. I was not interested in those machines attached to the wall that were variously designed to swallow pennies with little hope of reward. I expected more than this for my money, so I made for the football and hockey machines where you worked the handles and could prolong the game for minutes on end. The hall even possessed a large ingenious machine on which you could actually play baseball, a type I have never seen elsewhere.

Near the Palace Pier were the Aquarium and the Brighton Pavilion and the Dome, its former stables. I was never taken into the Pavilion or the Dome when I was a boy but I was taken for a treat to the Ice Stadium to see my first ice-hockey game: Brighton Tigers against Nottingham Panthers. In due course, I actually took to the ice myself one afternoon but it proved a sad disappointment. As a competent roller skater I started confidently, believing that all would be straightforward. Not so. I think I must have an antipathy to ice; to begin with I could not stand up straight on the blades of my skates, and when I attempted to move gracefully forward across the rink in my best Bloomfield Road style, I found that the skates were at a curious angle to my legs and my legs were at odds with my body. It was not a pretty sight, and two heavy falls quickly convinced me that I should stick to wheels.

I suppose I was lucky in having close relations in two such delightful and different places, although I know my friends had relations in equally attractive areas. Over the years visiting East Grinstead I learned to appreciate the pleasures of the countryside, but I am certain that for children the seaside has the more powerful appeal. The seaside is so indelibly associated with the idea of holiday that even visits to the coast out of season lift the spirits and fill the mind with anticipated joys. To actually live by the sea, I thought as a child, would truly be heaven. Nothing has happened since to alter that early view.

There were, of course, other visits and days out from home. One of my more memorable trips was that favourite excursion for many Londoners on summer weekends, a cruise down the Thames to Southend on the paddle-steamer, the *Golden Eagle*. We did this once on a hot Saturday in August. We took our usual picnic and enjoyed the novelty of a cruise in a sizeable vessel on a busy river. We disembarked at Southend and walked along the front until we found a comfortable spot on the beach. Determined to make the most of such an outing, I quickly changed into my swimming costume and hobbled across the shingle and into the water. Once my feet touched sand, I waded out until the water was chest-high. Then I turned and waved to my parents. 'Watch me!' I shouted and ducked under the water. When I came up I found I was covered from head to foot in oily slime. I waded miserably back to the beach and had to be taken to the nearest public lavatory to be washed down. This removed the worst of the oil but I was not properly clean until I reached home and had a hot bath that evening. Adieu, Southend! We never went again.

FOURTEEN

SACRED & PROFANE

'Happy, happy Christmas, that can win us back to the
delusions of our childish days.'

The Pickwick Papers, Dickens

Our household had a weekly rhythm determined by my mother's
activities. Sunday, however, as in most homes, was a special day.
In our case, it certainly did not include excessive religious
observance, because my parents always had a lie-in on Sunday mornings
with the prospect of a fried breakfast to be followed by a roast dinner. But
for me, it meant putting on clean underclothes following the ritual weekly
bath and going reluctantly to Sunday school.

Before a late breakfast (the Bristows were notorious for their love of
bed) my mother laid out my clean vest, pants and stockings on my bed.
This was straightforward enough in summer, but I came to detest putting
on my winter woollen underwear. First, I quickly pulled on the hated
woollen vest, with short sleeves and buttons at the neck, which was very
itchy and uncomfortable. Next were my woollen pants, with loops
through which I threaded my braces to button on to my trousers. I
developed a stiff-armed, stiff-legged gait to keep the wool away from my
skin but it was ineffective. It took a good two days before I felt
comfortable and then it was almost time, or so it seemed, for the whole
process to be repeated the following Sunday. On top of this hair shirt I
wore a grey flannel shirt, school tie, grey short trousers, a sleeveless
pullover and a jacket. After Sunday dinner, well wrapped up in my school
mackintosh and scarf, I sallied forth to Sunday school with a penny in my
pocket for the collection.

My attendance at Sunday school needs a little elaboration. My father
had no interest at all in religion although he occasionally claimed that he
was 'chapel' by upbringing just to tease my mother. She was Church of
England, though she was only an occasional communicant at Christmas
and Easter. Despite being nominally C of E, I was regularly despatched to

Sunday school at whatever church or chapel happened to be nearest. So we never attended church as a family, but my parents, like so many, felt obliged to see that I made a passing acquaintance with religion. In Frederick Place I went to St James's Sunday school at the end of the road for a while until I was encouraged by a friend to join the Lifebuoys. As a result, I found myself in the Baptist chapel round the corner in Conduit Road. Here we sat in rows on wooden forms in a Spartan hall and roared out the old choruses such as, 'I will make you fishers of men'. I much preferred these to the rather lacklustre hymns I encountered at St James's.

On becoming a Lifebuoy I wore a blue jersey and a round naval cap and fell in one evening a week in the hall attached to the chapel. After prayers we were split into watches and were given instruction in basic seamanship, signalling, first aid and played slightly different but equally competitive games. It was not too dissimilar in essence from the Cubs, except for the obvious nautical flavour and the fact that we had at least musical instruction, if not a band. We squatted in front of a blackboard and were issued with tambourines and triangles; sadly I was always a triangle, never a tambourine. One of the officers took station by the blackboard and let go the music, which was printed on a huge sheet of cartridge paper. On the staves the notes for each instrument were indicated by colours. Our leader took his pointer, paused, and waited for silence. It fell. We sat cross-legged, hunched over our primitive instruments. Then the pointer began to move and when it reached our particular colour we responded as vigorously and accurately as we could. Out into the suburban night drifted the strains of our standard piece, Delibes' ballet music to *Sylvia*. I never hear it without thinking of our earnest music making.

The big boys in our unit, those who had ceased to be Lifebuoys and had moved onwards and upwards into the Boys' Brigade, wore a more sophisticated dress. It was not so much a uniform as trappings, for over their normal clothes they wore a white diagonal belt, with a white haversack and pouch, set off by a jaunty pillbox cap. Before I became a Lifebuoy, whenever we caught sight of any members of the Boys' Brigade, we used to taunt them, at a distance, with:

'Here comes the Boys' Brigade
All covered in marmalade.'

This, of course, had to stop when I started going round to Conduit Road. Our brigade had a drum and bugle band, which led us loudly through the streets on special occasions such as Armistice Day and Empire Day, when we joined forces with the Cubs, Scouts, Brownies and Guides for a service at a local church. I left the Lifebuoys when I went to

St Olave's because of the pressure of homework and other activities. Thus I had a varied religious upbringing. I am sure that if there had been a Roman Catholic church round the corner I would have found myself in danger of becoming an altar boy.

After the excitement of the summer holiday, the next special day to look forward to was Bonfire Night on 5 November. We tended to call it Bonfire Night rather than Guy Fawkes Night. I started saving up for my fireworks in early October and then, with about a week to go, I started making the guy – with a little assistance. We always had a bonfire and a proper guy and I think my parents enjoyed themselves as much as I did. My mother usually managed to conjure up an old pair of my father's trousers and a discarded jacket and I would stuff them with newspaper, rags or shavings. On this trunk I fixed a head, made out of a stuffed stocking, to which I fastened a mask bought from Sergeant's. The guy was topped off with a hat cadged from a relative or friend – there was a limit to the amount of old clothes my father could supply. My friends and I went to considerable trouble to make our guys as realistic as possible and they compared very favourably with the pathetic, shrunken creatures we saw slumped outside shops and public houses, attended by a couple of children accosting passers-by with, 'Penny for the guy, mister!' We never got involved with this; our guys were for internal consumption only.

My father built the bonfire in the middle of his small vegetable patch, first driving in the tall stake to which we could eventually secure the guy. We only took the guy out at the last minute in case he got soaked with rain. In London we did not have any parkin or treacle toffee, those traditional accompaniments to Bonfire Night in the north. On the night, the three of us trooped out into the dark after tea and then the fun started. Rockets were already shooting up into the night sky and one or two bonfires were burning near us. I started off with sparklers, waving them in the air and dancing round the pyre, and worked up through squibs, Roman candles, Silver and Golden Rain, Mount Vesuvius/Etna to Catherine wheels, pinned to one of the washing-line posts. I finished with a few real bangers and a couple of rockets (which were relatively expensive) set off in a milk bottle. Then the moment came for lighting the bonfire. I watched fascinated as the flames took hold and licked round my father's old grey flannels. Slowly, the guy was consumed by the blaze; the string holding him to the stake burned through and hat, head and torso slumped forward into the fire.

By now there were several bonfires blazing in gardens along our road and small black figures, fitfully silhouetted against the flames, danced in the gloom. The night sky around us glowed at many points with the reflection of the fires; occasionally great bursts of sparks would leap upwards over a rooftop, or a shower of stars from an expiring rocket would float down for a few seconds until lost in the darkness. Our guy was now almost reduced to ashes; a few coat and trouser buttons and strips of burnt cloth were all that was left of our mannikin. We made our way indoors, rather grubby and smelling of smoke. Outside there was still the occasional bang and the whoosh of a rocket but the children's cries were fainter now and the red glow in the sky had begun to fade. What an evening! What a Bonfire Night!

The next morning, I went out into the garden and picked at the ashes of the bonfire with a stick. I collected up burnt sparklers, the sodden remains of bangers and the wooden handles of Roman candles. The red centre of the last Catherine wheel, still held by its pin, hung exhausted on the post. Sometimes in the wet grass or on the flower beds I found the stick and charred casing of a rocket fired from a neighbour's garden. All over for another whole year, a pleasing melancholy descended upon me.

At the beginning of December the shadow of Christmas fell across our house and the preparations began. I cannot at this point isolate any one particular Christmas and describe it. The Christmases of my boyhood merge in memory into one longed-for, happy festival of eating, games, chocolates and presents – the climax of the year.

There is, however, an exception. For two years running, in the mid-1930s, we entertained members of my mother's family for two or three days over Christmas. There were aunts and uncles sleeping on camp beds and on the floors of the bedrooms, and even on the settee in that holy of holies, the front room. How the dozen of us managed to wash, shave and dress I do not remember – I think a rather communal spirit was abroad. What I do remember, and my parents used to refer to this at every Christmas until their deaths, was that my father arranged for a 'poor woman' to come in on Christmas Day and Boxing Day to wash up after dinner. My father secretly enjoyed seeing himself, if only fleetingly, as an employer.

Well before the great day, I presented Father Christmas with a short list of what I would like for Christmas. We did not put this up the chimney for him to collect because of the fire burning in the grate but left it instead on the mantelpiece. He managed to find it just the same, for it was gone when I came down in the morning. He never disappointed me.

I looked forward to going round the brightly lit and decorated shops in Powis Street and Hare Street with my mother, doing some of the pre-Christmas shopping. An understood treat was a visit to a bazaar offered by one of the stores and we usually went to Garrett's. In the store we passed into an elaborate grotto – it could be Fairyland, Aladdin's Cave or a Pirate's Lair – and emerged the other side to meet Father Christmas. To be honest, I was not really fussed about meeting him; all I wanted was to get out as soon as possible and unwrap the parcel he gave me. Once or twice we went on the tram to Peckham Rye to do some special shopping, perhaps to buy a coat or dress for my mother. There were two stores in Peckham with bazaars, but the better one by far was that of Jones & Higgins – a more imaginative grotto and a better class of present!

It must have been in one of these stores that I first came across the network of cash-railways that were a feature of many of the large stores then. When you bought something, the shop assistant wrote out a bill, wrapped your money in it, reached up above her head and screwed it into a small wooden container. She then pulled down a handle, releasing a spring, which rang a bell and sent the canister whizzing unsteadily along its wires to the cashier's desk. The cashier removed the money, inserted the change, and sent the container scurrying back from whence it came.

In this period, just before Christmas, the atmosphere in both my infant and my junior school was similar to that when the end-of-term exams were over. There was a relaxation of tension, a time for private reading, word games and spelling bees. We made paper-chains and decorations amid a scarcely suppressed excitement about the approaching holiday and the various pleasures to come. In both schools, the classrooms, even in Mr Williams's top class, were decorated with paper-chains and streamers while a Christmas tree suddenly appeared in the hall. Cyril Bull conducted the carol service and I am sure he and the other teachers pretended not to hear us singing the lively:

> 'We three kings of Garrett's bazaar,
> Selling soap at two pence a bar.'

Followed by:

> 'While shepherds washed their socks by night.'

They must have seen us smirking at each other, though.

On Christmas Eve I went reluctantly to bed. There was no question of hanging a sock up; in view of my numerous relatives it was always a pillowcase hung invitingly open from the end of my bed. My mother tucked me in, kissed me goodnight and, like parents everywhere, whispered, 'Now, remember, Father Christmas won't come until you're fast asleep.' I do not think there is anything in childhood to equal the excitement of waking up on Christmas morning to find that Father Christmas has been. I opened my eyes and saw my pillowcase crammed with presents; there were parcels overflowing on to my bed – I could feel them with my feet. I sat up and tore at the string and brown paper (there was no fancy wrapping paper then) while my mother tried to restrain me with, 'Let's see who it's from first.' Although my 'big' present naturally came from my parents, my many aunts and uncles were unfailingly generous to their eldest nephew. 2s 6d would buy a good quality present: boxes of soldiers, jigsaws, annuals, conjuring and chemistry sets, Meccano, and games of all kinds. If looked after, and as an only child I was able to look after my possessions, they would last for years. By the time I had reached the bottom of my pillowcase, I was sitting up in a sea of brown paper, boxes and presents.

My parents rarely failed to point out at this moment that when they were young, all they and their brothers and sisters had in their stockings was an apple or an orange, a bright new penny and a bag of sweets. I thought they were joking but I realise now that it was true. For them this would be at the end of the nineteenth century and in the early years of the twentieth. In general, present-giving at Christmas to children of poor working-class families did not develop, even on a very modest scale, until a little before the First World War with the arrival of Woolworths and the era of cheap, mass-produced toys.

Playing with my presents made the morning slip away and soon it was time for the best meal of the year, Christmas dinner. This was either roast chicken or roast turkey (if there was a crowd of us) with all the trimmings: roast potatoes, sprouts, bread sauce and thick, delicious gravy. After a decent interval, a Christmas pudding appeared, dark and rich, studded with hidden threepenny pieces – 'threepenny joeys' my parents called them. I did not particularly care for this type of pudding and I liked even less the white sauce my mother poured over it. Even so, I still had a small slice in the hope of getting a threepenny bit and, strangely enough, I always managed to find one. Wine drinking played no part in our lifestyle so the ladies had soft drinks with their meal, although Nana had a Guinness, while the men had bottles of beer. Later my father produced a bottle of port to accompany the nuts, dates and Turkish Delight. Then we pulled our crackers, put on our paper hats, read out our mottoes and eased our chairs back from the table.

Eventually, we cleared the debris and settled down round the fire to listen to King George V's Christmas message on the wireless and pass round the chocolates. Before you could turn round, it was time to move into the front room for tea and the rest of the day. Tea was a mild affair centred round the Christmas cake. About two months before I had been present at the making of this on the living-room table, where much of my mother's food preparation was done as she had no proper working surface in the scullery. My father and I had the traditional three stirs of the unlikely looking mixture and made our secret wish. Then the contents vanished, to reappear transmogrified for Christmas tea, iced, decorated and befrilled. I did not like Christmas cake much either. To me it seemed like solidified Christmas pudding, covered with a thick layer of almond paste and topped with icing like thin slate. I did say I was difficult about food.

I was allowed to stay up a little later over Christmas and after tea we played cards and games until it was time for me to go upstairs. I got quickly into bed and lay there, warm and full and happy, soon lulled to sleep by the distant chatter and laughter downstairs where they were preparing an elaborate cold supper.

On Boxing Day it was more of the same, except that it would be cold meats for several more meals until the turkey or chicken appeared in curries and finally disappeared into soup. In the afternoon there was sometimes a special treat for me, a visit to the pantomime. We went every year, but where we went depended on circumstances. How I looked forward to it! When I was small, we walked to the Royal Artillery Theatre; then in the mid-1930s we started going up to London for our pantomime, to the Lyceum to see Clarkson Rose, a famous dame. This was my first experience of sitting anywhere in a theatre other than the pit-stalls. We must have sat in the upper circle because I was quite unnerved, like my mother, by the steep rake of the auditorium. I wondered what would happen to me if I stumbled and tumbled down the stairs with only a flimsy brass rail between me and the vast gulf of the stalls. I often wonder if any small child or elderly relative ever met a theatrical end by plunging head first over the rail on to the heads of those in the dress circle or down into the blackness of the pit. Since this was a special occasion, we had a small box of chocolates and ice creams for three during the interval.

When I think back to those pre-war Christmasses in Frederick Place, several cameos spring vividly to life, most of them associated with times when we had members of the family staying with us. I can see tiny, plump Uncle Reg sitting in the best chair by the fire, drinking a second glass of port and cracking his way steadily through a large bowl of mixed nuts. My father did not care greatly for Reg because he was 'red-hot Labour' – Labour was always 'red-hot' to my parents. Also, as I learned later, he was a 'great one for the horses' and a rather unsuccessful one at that. It was Reg's devotion to the turf that enabled him to get on so well with Nana. More to the point, perhaps, my father rarely drank and then it was only a modest half pint of bitter or a bottle of pale ale. Reg always drank gin, so whenever they went out together for a drink the disparity in cost always irritated my amiable father.

Nana.

Auntie Glad.

I remember Nana and Auntie Glad, both steely-eyed and smoking furiously, sitting round the table playing solo, nap, Newmarket and whist without giving an inch. I watched them playing for hours on end for halfpennies and pennies, critical of the hands they were dealt, piqued if they lost, and given to faintly hostile post-mortems. As always, my mother and her sisters would be washing up in the scullery in a mist of steam and warm family talk. Ah, times past, indeed. How we all wish we could rub that wonderful lamp and return for a little time to simple scenes like those.

FIFTEEN

EVENING ENTERTAINMENTS

'Dreams, books, are each a world; and books, we know,
Are a substantial world, both pure and good:
Round them, with tendrils strong as flesh and blood,
Our pastime and our happiness will grow.'

Personal Talk, Wordsworth

You may wonder how I spent my evenings in those distant, pre-war, pre-television days. In summer, the answer is simple – playing out with my friends. While I was at Fox Hill, I usually played in the street until it was time for tea; in my St Olave's years, when I had finished my homework, I would go out to play either in the streets or up on Plumstead Common until it was time for bed.

One feature of those summer evenings was the walks my parents and I used to take, especially at weekends. Going for walks with your parents was quite a normal and accepted occurrence; all my friends did this. We would often stroll up to Plumstead Common after tea and spend some time listening to the band before going on to watch the cricket. It would also give my parents the opportunity to admire or criticise the front gardens of the houses we passed. Since our route home took us past the houses of friends we would sometimes call in for a casual and genial half-hour. At weekends we tended to go a little further afield. We would set off up Plum Lane and Shrewsbury Lane to the top of Shooter's Hill, cross the old Dover Road and wander in the woods there, a popular area for family walks, especially in warm weather. When I was a little older, my parents used to round off our walk with a visit to the putting green in Castle Woods. Afterwards we would stroll contentedly through the woods past the ruins of Severndroog Castle and so back home in the twilight.

When the leaves fell from the trees and the evenings began to draw in, the pattern of my evenings changed. I no longer played out with friends, except at the weekends, and I tended to concentrate on my winter interests. There were stamps to be stuck in, soldiers to be organised and board games to be played, but more and more of my time was spent reading, curled up in the old basket chair or lying flat on my stomach on the hearth rug by the fire. I became a voracious reader, though I am embarrassed not to be able to recall more accurately what I read and at what age I read it. Encouraged by staff at Fox Hill, I joined the junior section of the Woolwich public library and was quickly immersed in the stories of Henty, Ballantyre, Gunby Hadath and Percy Westerman. *Treasure Island*, *Robinson Crusoe*, and *Gulliver's Travels* became firm favourites. I also read parts of *David Copperfield* and *Oliver Twist* but I cannot remember if I read these books in the original or in a special children's edition; I suspect the latter. I suppose my favourite reading in the late 1930s was the *Just William* books of Richmal Crompton. The middle-class background to the stories – cooks and maids, large gardens, tennis parties, cars – seemed far away from my own, though less distant than the country house settings of many crime novels and those curious public schools which formed part of my reading. Even so, it was easy to identify with William and Ginger and Henry and Douglas, while Violet Elizabeth was the epitome of soppy girls.

For Christmas and birthday presents I was often given annuals. In the 1930s, these were not comic-strip annuals (although there were one or two such as *Film Fun*) but collections of stories about public-school life, the First World War, the sea, exciting tales of uprisings in Africa and restless tribes on the Indian frontier, of pirates and explorers, Cavaliers and Roundheads, and, of course, Robin Hood. I lived in an imaginary world of action, excitement and romance where heroes battled against great odds, often assisted by plucky young lads, and where villains, usually swarthy foreigners, were outwitted at the last and met a well-deserved fate.

I browsed, too, among my parents' few books, Edwardian prizes for school attendance and Sunday school attendance. These contained exciting accounts of heroic deeds in the service of the Empire. There were blood-curdling stories about the Indian Mutiny and fights in the Sudan, with much emphasis on the Victoria Crosses awarded for the defence of Rorke's Drift and the more recent battles of the Boer War.

Comics, too, were a significant part of my reading, though the title 'comics' is a misnomer for they were essentially boys' magazines or 'story papers'. Those comics, which told stories in strip cartoon form with speech balloons, such as *Film Fun* and *Dandy* (first published in 1937), we despised and rarely looked at. We read the big five comics which cost 2*d* and were published weekly. Their ranking in terms of popularity was: the

Wizard, the *Hotspur*, the *Rover*, the *Adventure*, and the *Skipper*, with the first two well out in front. I started off with the *Wizard* but eventually became a devotee of the *Hotspur*, which contained a famous serial about the boys of Red Circle School and the odious form master, Mr Smugg.

We did not read the *Magnet* or the *Gem* although we were aware of them. I very occasionally saw a copy of the *Magnet* but I found the public-school caperings of Billy Bunter (Yarooh!) and his love/hate relationship with Harry Wharton and the Greyfriars crew neither exciting nor compelling. I wanted a more varied and heady diet. I suspect that about this time the *Magnet* was on the wane and the *Gem* had had its day. Certainly I saw few copies of either at St Olave's and both magazines were abruptly closed down soon after the outbreak of war.

This colourful and romantic reading affected my character and attitudes in a number of ways, several of which only became apparent in adolescence. Not being a young gentleman as such, and having standards of gentility, if not exactly thrust upon me at home, at least held up for admiration and imitation, I conceived from my reading by the age of thirteen a quaint olde-worlde code of honour and morality. Courtesy and chivalry to women were paramount, of course – though sadly in my case, women did not appear to include mothers. To one's friends, unswerving loyalty was the rule; this included taking the blame (unfairly, naturally) rather than give away one's chums. With this went a refusal to stoop to do anything at all underhand – 'gentlemen don't do such things.'

This knightly code of conduct was exemplified in the playing of games, particularly cricket. Having given one's opponent every advantage, including the benefit of the doubt, one should then strive vigorously to win. One should be modest in victory and gracious in defeat; any game, if winning involved infringing the spirit or relying overmuch on the letter of the law, was simply not worth the playing. At all times, one had to play the game.

My fictional diet also bred in me a romantic attachment to what I saw as matters of principle, resulting in a dogged refusal to bend and a willingness to be in a minority of one, which proved rather uncomfortable in practice. As you can see, I had all the makings of a proper little prig. I find it embarrassing to recount all this, and at the same time to realise how short I fell of the more admirable of these qualities in later life.

I wish I could remember if we took a daily paper regularly during our years at Frederick Place. I don't think we did but my father sometimes brought home a copy of the *Evening News*. You may feel it strange that I remained so unaware of events in Europe in the mid- to late 1930s. I listened at times with half an ear to the news on the wireless and I suppose I must have seen headlines and pictures in the papers and newsreels in the cinema, but I had the much more pressing concerns of boyhood and school life to contend with. My father was not particularly interested in politics or foreign affairs, and I can remember no political discussions going on in our house. I cannot remember seeing banner headlines about Hitler, Abyssinia and Munich, probably because at my age I was not interested in what was going on in Europe and Africa. My friends and I regarded Hitler and Mussolini as comic figures and were amused by their posturing, rhetoric and funny salutes; we used to go around goose-stepping and 'Heil Hitler!'-ing each other. To be honest, I do not think I was conscious of Mussolini's activities, the Spanish Civil War or the significance of Czechoslovakia – though I could spell it at the drop of a hat! It was not until the early months of 1939 that I became dimly aware of the possibility of war.

Both my parents were Conservatives, like all their friends and relatives. My mother had no interest in politics and voted Conservative simply because it enabled her to identify with a class she admired and had once served. I think she regarded it as a further sign of refinement; 'Yes, dear, we always vote Conservative,' she would say to me contentedly. My father, who came from a rural and traditionally conservative background, voted Tory from a conviction born of habit. He was by upbringing deferential to what he regarded as a naturally ruling class and he regarded the 'Labourites' (his term), with whom his work brought him into contact in London, with some disdain. Besides, voting Conservative reflected his recently acquired status as an owner-occupier and his place in a property-owning democracy.

We did, however, have the local weekly paper, the *Kentish Independent*, a title which reminded us that Woolwich and Plumstead, before becoming part of the administrative County of London, were in Kent. On Sundays we took the *News of the World*. I never read this (which was just as well, perhaps, for otherwise I might have shied away from becoming either a choirboy or a scout), except to glance at its football page with league tables and forecasts when my father filled in his Littlewoods Pools coupon on Wednesday evenings. This was a regular feature of his week; although he never won more than a few shillings on a couple of occasions, it did not stop us dreaming of the big win and discussing how we would spend the money.

During the winter evenings we often listened to the wireless, as it was universally known. Even today, I refer naturally to 'the wireless'; I find it hard, and I have to make a conscious effort, to say 'radio' – such prisoners are we of our childhood. My father had bought one of the first crystal sets, complete with headphones and cable in a stout mahogany box. He assembled it on the table and we took it in turns to listen to this new marvel, trying hard to remain still and keep the cat's whisker on the crystal. The novelty of this, given the unsatisfactory reception, soon wore off. However, radio was making giant strides and we soon had our first proper wireless set, a valve set with an accumulator and a dry battery, and a loud speaker, which enabled the family to listen in together. The accumulator, which was about a quarter the size of a modern car battery, was cased in glass and carried in a metal frame with a wooden handle. It needed recharging from time to time, so my father and I would walk down Burrage Road to the corner of Crescent Road to a tiny shop run by a small hunchback with a club foot. The shop was full of the acrid smell of acid. The hunchback took our accumulator, dragged himself from the counter to the banks of accumulators at the rear, put it on charge, and handed us a fully charged one in return.

I suppose I gradually became aware of the wireless from the mid-1930s. I used to come home from school, settle down in the basket chair and listen regularly to *Children's Hour* with Uncle Mac. By far my favourite programme was *Toytown*, with its unforgettable range of characters, each with its distinctive, individual voice: Mr Mayor, Larry the Lamb, Ernest the Policeman, the Inventor and Dennis the Dachshund. I also liked the Ovalteenies on Radio Luxembourg, the not-quite respectable commercial station, with their club, badge and famous song:

> 'We are the Ovalteenies,
> Happy girls and boys . . .'

My parents listened to the six o'clock news (this was to become a fetish with them during the war), but it had virtually no interest for me. I cannot remember listening to any football commentaries (rugby was an unknown world to me then) but I used to take down the football results after the news on Saturday afternoons, so that my father could check his pools coupon. The only sporting outside broadcasts I do recall listening to with my father were the fights between the two heavyweights, our own Jack Petersen and the German, Walter Neusel. Of all the family programmes, the one I enjoyed most was *Music Hall*, partly because it was transmitted on Saturday nights and I was allowed to stay up a little later to hear it. I did not care much for the solo singers, genteel sopranos and reverberating baritones, or for the popular duettists of the day. It was the comedians I liked, and the names of those artists are like a roll of honour of the final days of the music hall. These were robust and powerful personalities toughened and honed in the rough and tumble of the twice-nightly variety theatres.

Although I promised myself not to indulge in lists, my heart tells me I must mention George Robey, Albert Whelan, Harry Tate, the Western

Brothers (Kenneth and George), Robb Wilton, Gert and Daisy (Elsie and Doris Walters), Harry Champion, Max Miller, the Two Leslies, Tommy Handley and George Formby; also the comediennes, Florrie Forde, Hetty King, Nellie Wallace and, above all, Gracie Fields. I never saw any of these artists on the stage, except Max Miller, and I realise how much of the art and impact of their acts was lost on the wireless. My mother considered Max Miller 'rather blue', though she seemed to enjoy his stand-up routines, shyly glancing towards my father or her sisters. 'Blue' he certainly was in the theatre, but what a performer! I find it sad that the names of the great stars and the songs they sang mean virtually nothing today. The name of Gracie Fields may awaken a faint echo, but silence cloaks the rest.

My parents had seen many of the popular figures of the music hall on visits to the theatre during the war and in the 1920s, and my childhood echoed to the songs made famous by the stars from the turn of the century. My parents also sang the sentimental and cynical songs of the First World War. The other strands in my parents' musical background were melodies from the Edwardian musical comedies of their youth and one or two songs from the Boer War. These various elements composed their musical culture, and I absorbed this. On the infrequent occasions when my relatives found themselves gathered round a piano, it was always to the old songs of their youth and the war they returned. I may have been somewhat contemptuous of much of it later on, but the melodies won in the end, and they still spring unbidden to my mind.

Television appeared in the mid-1930s, but nobody we knew had a set. I remember seeing the tiny screens at the top of what seemed enormous consoles when they first appeared in the shops. There was a wireless shop at the top of Anglesea Road and we used to stop for a few moments on our way down to the shops in Woolwich to watch the flickering black and white pictures.

Near the bandstand on Plumstead Common and on the corner of Blendon Road stood the Globe cinema, where I first went to the pictures. I am not saying that going to the cinema was a regular winter pursuit of mine (far from it) but the three of us did go occasionally and it seems sensible to deal with it here. I still tend to talk of 'going to the pictures' unless, yet again, I make a conscious effort to say or write, 'to the cinema'; we never said going to the 'flicks' or to the 'movies'. My parents always referred to going to the 'picture palace' which, on reflection, seems a delightful title. The Globe had originally been built as a chapel and was nothing more than a lofty, rectangular box with a narrow balcony. It was lit at first by a few gas globes down each side and had, despite a half-hearted attempt at upholstery, seats of unrelenting hardness. My mother first took me to an occasional matinee there from Herbert Road when I was an infant and was thus admitted free. In later years, my parents would take me in winter on a Saturday afternoon or sometimes in the evening when there was what they called a 'good' film on. This meant a historical or literary drama: we saw Charles Laughton in *Mutiny on the Bounty*, *The Private Life of Henry VIII* and *Rembrandt*; George Arliss (a favourite of my parents) in *Disraeli* and *Cardinal Richlieu, David Copperfield* and *Treasure Island*. At a less exalted level we enjoyed Douglas Fairbanks in *The Man in the Iron Mask*, and Alan Jones in *The Firefly* – I sang the Donkey Serenade for ages afterwards. Another musical number which caught my imagination (and friends still sing it jokingly today) was the canoe song from *Sanders of the River*. You certainly had your money's worth in those days; the programme lasted about three hours and, besides the big picture, included a supporting 'B' picture, *Pathé Gazette* (a news film) and a cartoon.

Need I add that the films my friends and I saw, with their pirates, cavaliers, cowboys, soldiers, athletic swordsmen and Indians, fired our imaginations and provided the basis for many of our chasing and attacking games? We fully identified with these heroes.

In April 1937, the Granada cinema opened at the bottom of Powis Street; this was the period of the building of opulent suburban cinemas. The *Kentish Independent* declared it to be 'the most romantic cinema ever built, with its wall of mirrors and cathedral atmosphere.' It was designed in the Continental-Gothic style and decorated by Theodore Komisarjevsky of the Moscow Arts Theatre. With its Moorish arches and filigree panels it evoked the warmth and romance of southern Spain and set hitherto undreamed-of standards of comfort and luxury. I remember my father taking us to the opening night there. The Mayor of Woolwich officiated and the opening ceremony was performed by the glamorous West End star, Frances Day, in a sheath of burgundy velvet and a halo of platinum-blonde hair. I was eleven years old and felt stirrings above my age and station. The main attraction (after Francis Day) was Will Hay in the film, *Good Morning, Boys*, supported by Reginald Dixon at the enormous organ – always referred to as 'the mighty Wurlitzer'. Woolwich had seen nothing like the Granada; we succumbed to its palatial charms and transferred our allegiance from the humble Globe.

Later in the same year, a rival cinema opened opposite the Granada. One of the Odeon chain being built in the suburbs, this one was designed by George Coles in the curvy faience style. Again, it had a most impressive interior with, to our minds, opulent seating and a café upstairs. It also, of course, had an organ. Cinema organs were a major attraction of the new cinemas and a few organists became national celebrities, appearing on the music halls and on the BBC. It was a new and exciting experience for the audience. After the interval, the lights dimmed, the opening chords welled up from the darkness, and then, up from the orchestra pit, picked out in a blaze of light, rose the mighty Wurlitzer. At the organ sat the maestro in a dazzling white suit, fluttering his fingers across the several keyboards, dancing his feet along the pedals and smiling a gleaming smile over his shoulder. I was unaffected by all this – I was simply impatient for the next picture to start.

Such was the pattern of my activities on winter evenings; homework, reading, games, the wireless and the very occasional visit to the cinema. Although my parents were always willing to play with me after tea, inevitably I was forced in upon myself a great deal. I spent long hours playing alone. This did not worry me unduly and I rarely felt lonely. Life had always been like that. It did mean, however, that I grew up a self-centred and introspective child, one accustomed to, and content with, his own company and pursuing his own interests. I was a boy who spent a great deal of time reading and who lived much in the world of the imagination. Yet, although I was secure and happy after my own fashion, the nature of this childhood, aggravated by the fact that I was an only child who had a little too much of his own way ('spoilt' my relatives called me, and they should know!), was to scar my adolescence.

SIXTEEN

IN A LARGE POND

'I only know two sorts of boys, mealy boys and beef-faced boys.'
Oliver Twist, Charles Dickens

In the early summer of 1937 I was among those chosen from the top class to sit the 'scholarship' exam. If you passed, you were able to enter one of the LCC's maintained grammar schools. Your parents could choose, with Cyril Bull's guidance, from a list of grammar schools which included Colfe's, the Roan, St Olave's, City of London and Aske's among others. It had been intimated to several of us in Mr Williams's class that we stood a very good chance of winning a scholarship, so we sat the examination in the hall with a certain amount of nervous tension but with some confidence.

All went well on the day and I duly passed to become the first generation grammar school boy in the family, and years later the first university graduate. My parents were delighted, the school took my photograph, and I was soon among those faces on the wall in the hall. The head advised us to apply for admission to St Olave's and St Saviour's Grammar School in Tooley Street, Southwark. This, he said, was a crack London academic grammar school with a new head, Dr R.C. Carrington, where several Fox Hill boys had already done very well. So I applied to 'Stogs', as it was nicknamed, and so did my friends, Alan Peters, David Doig and Gerald Plaistow, and we were all accepted on Cyril Bull's recommendation.

A few boys, who had failed the examination but had performed creditably, went to the Central School in Bloomfield Road to do a commercial course. Bloomfield Road, originally an ordinary senior school, had been one of those selected for development some years before as higher elementary schools. This experiment proved successful, and now under their new title of 'central schools' they provided a limited range of vocationally biased courses. The rest of my class, the majority, left for the senior school in Plum Lane where they would stay until they reached the school-leaving age of fourteen.

St Olave's Grammar School, Tooley Street.

Although I sensed that I had reached and passed an educational milestone, I did not realise the changes to my life that going to St Olave's would bring. I knew that, apart from Alan, David and Gerald, I would know nobody in a school that drew its pupils from all over South London. I was dimly aware that competition in a form (not 'class' any more) composed entirely of scholarship boys would be fierce, and that I should now have homework to do every evening before thinking of going out to play. I did not appreciate that I would inevitably lose touch with those classmates who were going to other schools, and that travelling to London, homework, new friends and activities would draw me away from the friends I had grown up with in the street. I was not unduly troubled at the prospect of leaving my small pond for unknown Southwark, but I did not realise that this was the beginning of a slow and remorseless process which was to lever me from my roots in south-east London and steadily distance me from my parents. All this was in the future. Those of us who were going to grammar schools left Fox Hill with the congratulations and good wishes of Cyril Bull and his staff loud in our ears.

For the rest of that summer I was in a kind of limbo. I had not quite severed my ties with Fox Hill because at the end of term there was one last enjoyable school journey to the Isle of Wight. Once we had returned, however, I knew that my happy days at Fox Hill were over and that before me a path wound into an unknown future. A family holiday at Bognor helped to bridge the gap, and then, suddenly, it was time to get me ready for my new school in September.

In August, my father received a leaflet from St Olave's setting out the details of the curriculum, school uniform, games kit and other helpful information under such headings as 'sanitary precautions', 'homework' and 'Head's consultation hours'. Thus 'The Head is prepared to see parents for Consultation on Monday, Tuesday, or Thursday, between 11.00 and 11.45 – and at other times by previous appointment: but he is not at liberty on Wednesday'. One wonders idly what was so special about Wednesdays and the nature of his activities. Under 'dinner', and emphasised in italics, I read with a frisson of alarm: 'A good meal in the middle of the day is a necessity for growing boys.' The uniform requirements were not very demanding; we had to buy a cap and tie and there was a wire badge to be sewn onto the breast pocket if we chose to

The hall at St Olave's.

wear a blazer. I was to discover that while a number of us wore grey suits, plain or patterned, others wore blazers or blue serge suits – blue serge seemed popular with boys who lived nearby in Southwark or Bermondsey. The most curious item of dress, about which I had heard rumours some months before, was a stiff white Eton collar. These collars were a curious survival; they were rapidly going out of fashion (they were to disappear within two years of the war) and were worn outside the collars of our jackets. They were made either of linen, which had to be laundered, or a kind of celluloid which could be cleaned with a damp rag. With these collars we had to wear a white shirt and a school tie, either a club tie or a square-ended narrow one. Such collars, which gave a faintly Victorian flavour to our appearance, were obligatory in the lower and upper fourths; once in the lower fifth, however, soft white collars were worn, though the giddy heights of the lower fifth were light years away at this point.

But the strangest item on the list of essentials was a copy of the School Hymnal. This had to be obtained from the school secretary and cost 5s, which we thought was rather expensive for a mere book of hymns. Not only that, this hymnal had to be covered in black hopsack, a coarse material with a loose weave; no other colour or cloth was acceptable. It was only later, as the term wore on, that I realised what a bizarre volume it was. Created by an early headmaster, a classical scholar full of Victorian moral fervour, I have never seen anything like it either before or since. It must have given him immense pleasure to compile it and introduce it into the school: after all, who would oppose a grammar school headmaster? On each page below the number was an appropriate biblical quotation followed by the hymn, with brief quotations and comments running down each margin. At the bottom of the page were poetic excerpts (much Tennyson), aphorisms and more quotations from a variety of authors, ancient and modern, known and unknown, including such strange bedfellows as Homer, Eliza Scudder (who she?), Gladstone and Spurgeon. These quotations came in many tongues: Latin, Greek, German, Italian, French, and in many types of fonts of varying sizes. Heavy Gothic rubbed shoulders with light italic, and block capitals vied with Greek (capitals and lower case). It must have been a typesetter's nightmare and close to exhausting the patience of the Cambridge University Press.

When I started at St Olave's in the autumn I had to make my way down to Woolwich Arsenal station, near Beresford Square, catch the train to London Bridge, and then walk half a mile along Tooley Street to my new school. Looking back, I am surprised by the equanimity with which my parents and I accepted the need for me, at the age of eleven, to become a junior commuter in the rush hour, and to travel up to London by train for the next seven years. There was little discussion and less fuss. It had been decided that I should go to St Olave's, and to get there it was necessary to travel up to London by train, so my father went down to Woolwich Arsenal and bought a special scholar's season ticket. It was as simple and uncomplicated as that. And so, on a bright morning in early September, I walked down to the station, flashed my new season ticket, met my three friends on the platform, caught the 8.20 and steamed off to a new life.

At London Bridge station we piled out of the train, pushed through the barrier waving our season tickets and tumbled down the steep flight of steps into Tooley Street. In those days, Tooley Street still retained its Victorian flavour. On the north side it was lined with tall buildings and great warehouses giving on to the Thames. Through the high-arched gateways, high because of the towering loads the carters had to manoeuvre, we could see vast brick warehouses, six storeys high and grimed with the fog and soot of generations, rising from a sea of cobbles. Beyond, we caught glimpses of the slim masts and delicate rigging of the shipping at the wharves. Over all this hung the penetrating Tooley Street perfume, an acrid smell compounded of tannery, brewery and horse, for here the decline of the horse had been momentarily halted. Horse-drawn carts still held sway, though a cart is a grotesque understatement for some of the giants that lumbered up the street. Lords of all were the brewers' drays, powerful horses of seventeen hands slipping and stumbling over the greasy cobbles, and snorting clouds of steam in the raw river air.

Further along Tooley Street towards my school, the warehouses gave way to mean shops and blocks of decaying tenements, their lower windows barred and their sad interiors obscured by yellowing lace curtains, dank with grime.

Only one shop along the road had any attraction for me and this was the baker's. Their speciality was Nelson cake, a pot-pourri of yesterday's leftovers, studded with currants and baked in large shallow trays. This was sold at a penny per puddingy portion, and very good it was, too. Now and again I splashed out on a piece to supplement my packed dinner brought from home which unvaryingly consisted of two cheese sandwiches, made with cream crackers, and a Lyon's individual fruit pie. Those boys who for either financial or gastronomic reasons preferred to bring sandwiches ate them in the hall; the dining room was given over entirely to the more orthodox diners. I could, of course, have stayed for dinner if I had wanted to, but I could not stomach the thought of having to eat dishes at school which I rejected at home, so I opted out. This was a pity because the food at school was wholesome and the experience would have done me a power of good in more ways than one. Instead, I had to learn the hard way and it was evacuation in 1939 that finally put paid to my finicky habits.

St Olave's stood at the junction of Tooley Street and Queen Elizabeth Street in the shadow of Tower Bridge and looked across the Thames to the Tower of London. From the art room at the top of the new block we could see the bascules rising and descending on the bridge, and the masts and funnels of ships in London river. This did not strike us as romantic but, then, small boys are not very romantic creatures. The school was undoubtedly a handsome building with a long façade divided into three parts. The impressive, central three-storied block was built in 1894 of red brick with stone quoins and dressings, Corinthian pillars and large, elegant windows. It was crowned by a clock and bell tower. To its left was an ivy-covered building much in the same style with a central projection which housed the staircase. This building contained the woodwork and metalwork rooms on the first floor while on the second were the gymnasium and changing room. On the right of the central block was a small modern block of classrooms connected to the main building by a short covered way.

When I first entered the hall, it struck me as enormous. A great barrel-vaulted roof, an immense arch of white plaster and black beams, soared into the air and from it eight huge electric lamps hung by chains. These were only lit late on winter afternoons as the grey light darkened into night. Shining frostily high up in the gloom they lent to the hall cathedral-like qualities of mass and mystery. Tall windows dominated the side of the hall facing the road while on the other side doors led to the form rooms of those Olympians, the Sixth and Lower Sixth. Form room, classroom, either seems quite inadequate to describe the dwelling of these exalted creatures. They were men of seventeen and eighteen, clever, athletic, virile, and sophisticated beyond belief. That such beings were actually taught, were subjected to a timetable, to an academic routine similar to ours, was unthinkable, impious. Above, at first-floor level, a narrow balcony ran the length of the hall with the classrooms of less superior boys opening on to it. Curving round at the end it led to the organ, glued perilously on the far wall, high above us. Below the organ, under the Royal arms, was the platform, empty save for the head's massive desk and his chair with the high Gothic back. Here, *solus*, glorious, monarch of all he surveyed, he took assembly.

In the corner of the hall by the side of the platform stood the war memorial inscribed with the names of those boys from the school who had fallen in the First World War, though at this time it held little significance for us. In the other corner were the main doors through which the Catholics and Jews, excluded from the morning service, marched in Indian file to join us after prayers to hear any announcements and homilies.

The hall was panelled in oak and on the panels, picked out in gold lettering, were the names, colleges and achievements of those who had

IN A LARGE POND

won their way to Oxford or Cambridge. Rather like the photographs on the wall at Fox Hill, their example shone down; a number of empty panels were still blank and the point was not lost upon us. Yet to us, 'university' was a far-off, unthinkable world, like marriage or work – proper work, I mean. The hall was permanently furnished with curious folding desks which I think were primarily designed for examination purposes. At prayers they hung limply as we stood in line abreast behind them; at dinner time they sprang into life when, with the top pulled up and locked into position, they served as tables for the sandwich boys.

At prayers, we stood facing the platform, junior forms in front and senior forms at the rear. From the smallest and youngest in the shadow of the throne, heads rose in a long, irregular slope towards the back of the hall: fair heads, black heads, here and there a red head, every shade of brown head, with hair lank, hair wavy, hair stubborn, hair greased. Smooth cheeks gave way to superfluous hair and this in turn surrendered to youthful stubble, while Eton collars yielded half way back to the soft white collars of the fifth. The masters, wrapped in their gowns, leaned like weary birds of prey against the panelling opposite their irresponsibilities.

At a signal, we fell silent. Then the head, gown billowing, entered the balcony from his room, passed in front of the organ and disappeared from sight as he descended the main staircase outside the hall. He reappeared through the entrance doors, mounted the platform, stood behind his desk and surveyed us. As my form was right in front of the platform, he towered above us; a youngish man, recently appointed, one of the coming men, classical scholar, noble Roman brow, he seemed at least 7ft tall. Directly beneath him stood the captain of the school and behind him, spaced out down the central aisle, the prefects, feet apart, hands clasped behind their backs. The captain of the school, demi-god, unapproachable, was a superb swimmer called Jack Hall who was to be killed in France in 1940. The head announced the hymn. Mr Cramp, the lame music master, attacked the organ and the school gave tongue. When the last notes had died away, one of the prefects came up onto the platform and read a passage of scripture. The head then led the prayers which I remember as being brief and to the point. Morning assembly was over. Dr Carrington gathered up his papers and his gown, gave us a withering glance and swept out, followed at a respectful distance by the prefects in line ahead. We were dismissed by forms and filed out to begin the day.

SEVENTEEN

TRANSPORTS
OF DELIGHT

'Two lads that thought there was no more behind
But such a day to-morrow as to-day
And to be boy eternal.'

The Winter's Tale, Shakespeare

I found myself in Lower IVB in a form room in the small modern block with thirty other boys, including my three Fox Hill friends. Our master was H.G. Wright, known as 'Dicky', a noted historian of the area round the school and notable for his invariable wing collar. On our first morning he compiled the register, and we had to give our surnames followed by our full Christian names and this caused some amusement. Nothing amused us as much as the name of one boy – Bugg, Ralph – who later became a close friend of mine. He had large, elaborate, semi-transparent ears, set at an angle to his skull, a thin, pointed nose with a prominent bridge, a wide grin, and a splay-footed running action that defies description. He was good-natured, eccentric, and generally accepted as a kind of child of nature. Sensibly, he made the best of a bad job and revelled in his name; it was, however, an embarrassment to others. It so happened that Dr Carrington chose to take us for scripture once a week. The first time he did so, he called the register: Alger, Boiling, Bristow, Brooks, and then he was brought up short by the ugly bluntness of Bugg. Not being a headmaster for nothing, and an Oxford man to boot, he paused only for a moment before declaring, 'Henceforth, you shall be called "Bewg"'. But the head was the only one who ever called him 'Bewg'; my chum remained stubbornly, unchangeably, Buggy.

In those days St Olave's was considered a large school. Besides Dr Carrington there was a second master, 'Bill' Whitton, a delightful classicist nearing retirement, and a staff of twenty-four. The academic staff were all graduates, four from Oxford, six from Cambridge, twelve from London and

Lower IVB with Dicky Wright.

one from Belfast; there were several scholars and exhibitioners among them and only a few were not trained teachers. I suppose the number of boys in the three-form entry school, including the small prep department, was about 480.

So, for the next two years I travelled up every morning on the 8.20 from Woolwich Arsenal. This train brought sober-suited office workers up to the City. It started life somewhere near Gravesend and, having fought its way up through the towns of north Kent, it was fairly crowded by the time it reached Woolwich Arsenal. As the covered part of the platform was lined with commuters, our little group used to gather at the far end of the platform, ready to infest the two rear carriages. These were always full of male quartets playing solo on newspapers stretched across their knees. We took much delight in bursting in upon them, forcing them to take up their cards and papers as we stumbled over shiny toecaps into the corridor. They used to curse us – and no wonder.

Once established in the corridor we whiled away the twenty minute journey in the traditional way, copying each other's homework, reciting irregular verbs, and hearing each other race through 'Earth has not anything to show more fair'. This may sound all very academic, but in fact it was accompanied by a great deal of background hiss, compounded of high-pitched squeals, shouts of laughter, a little mild song, and some scuffling. I suppose we were a pretty noisy bunch, but it was really nothing more than boyish animal spirits.

When the train was particularly full we were allowed to pile into the guard's van; on rare occasions we were able to scramble into the guard's van unobserved even when the train was far from full. I remember one morning when Vaughan, Bugg and I managed to slip in without being seen. The three of us made so much noise in the van during the journey that the passengers in the next compartment were reduced to drumming on the wooden panels between us and shouting for quiet. It was rather a pity that among those next door was Ladbrook, one of the school prefects. How we missed spotting him I do not know; we were not usually so lax. When the three of us stumbled out of the van on to the platform at London Bridge we were horrified to see Ladbrook waiting for us, flanked by a pair of angry travellers. Tall, severe, wearing his prefect's velvet cap and tassel, his usually amiable face set and stern, Ladbrook was short and to the point. 'What the devil do you think you're doing, kicking up all that row?' he barked. 'I shall report you to the head.' He turned on his heel and stalked off down the platform, leaving us deflated and apprehensive. The head! Phew! Would Ladbrook tell the head? He had always seemed rather a decent sort of chap; would he really report us?

He did; he had no option, of course. The summons came later that morning during chemistry. We were sitting on the worn, carved benches in the tiered lecture room at the top of the school listening to old Botty (young Mr Bott, the chemistry master) droning on about H_2SO_4. 'The head wishes to see Bugg and Bristow in his study at once.' My stomach seemed to drop away from my body. I dreaded chemistry; I had a mental block in this subject and old Botty always seemed to pick on me, but I left his class most reluctantly that morning. Of course, the whole class knew what it was about for the news had soon got round; our form mates sat there, hugging themselves, glad it was us and not them.

Buggy and I made our way to the empty hall, along the balcony and under the great organ, to the heavy outer oak door of the head's study. This was uninvitingly open. Nervously we stood outside. A few moments later we were joined by a white-faced Vaughan who was in Lower IVA. Vaughan was shivering, his lips trembled, and his eyes were bright with moisture. We waited a moment. 'Go on, knock,' said Buggy. As I raised my hand to knock on the inner door, from inside the head's room came a metallic clanging, shattering the stillness of the deserted hall. 'He's getting out the cane,' gasped Vaughan. In fact, he was poking the fire, but we were not to know this. Silence, an ominous silence. I knocked on the door. 'Come in,' snapped a voice. I gripped the large brass handle, turned it, and the door swung inwards. I had never been in the head's study before; few boys had. We stood in a quivering line in front of his desk. The head sat in his chair and fixed us with his eyes. He stared at us, he looked deep inside us, and what he saw displeased him. We cringed under that gaze. Vaughan shifted uneasily. 'Stand still, boy!' thundered the head. Vaughan jerked to attention like some marionette. Then the head began. In level, menacing tones he recounted the incident on the train, our lack of manners, our total lack of consideration for others, our disgraceful behaviour. We'll get six, I thought. We're bound to get six. We had let the school down; we had let him down. He paused, and then said slowly – I have always remembered his exact words – 'If you ever appear before me again for any reason whatsoever, while you're in this school, I shall thrash you. Now, get out!'

We got out. Unbelievable! We hadn't been whacked! It was too good to be true. Grinning and shaking with relief we went back to Botty. But the head had won; his words had seared our souls. None of us was ever reported to him again; at least, we were never caught again.

I suppose our favourite diversion on the way home was playing 'carriage – he'. Any number could play, but first you had to seize an empty compartment. This was easy for us because we came home before 4 p.m. when the trains from Charing Cross and Waterloo were practically empty, and no passenger in his right mind would choose to share his journey with six or seven lively boys who had been driven hard all day and were looking for outlets.

Once inside the compartment, one boy was chosen 'he' and blindfolded with a woolly school scarf. Then, while he stood with his face against the window at one end and counted up to twenty, the rest of us hid. To hide in an ordinary third-class railway compartment may sound odd, yet it is surprising the curious corners and spaces small boys can stow themselves away in. We hid underneath the seats (very filthy), on the luggage racks, and under the seat cushions; we even hung suspended above the carriage doors. When he reached twenty, 'he' turned and tried to catch and identify us while we took violent, evasive action – violent was the word. Whoever was caught then became 'he', and so it continued.

We could only play carriage-he in spasms for we had to stop whenever the train came to a station. We had to ensure that no one entered our compartment and we had this worked out to a fine art. As the train slid into the station, we flung the window down and four or five flushed faces peered out to deter any passengers waiting on the platform. It did the trick. Then, as the train gathered speed, the game was soon in full swing again.

We wanted an empty compartment also to enjoy the sensation of unbuttoned ease. Away from the scrutiny of adults, in the privacy of our third-class compartment, we could toss our satchels and cases where we liked, sprawl in the corners, put our feet up on the seats, laugh and talk and tease each other uninhibitedly. Surprisingly, perhaps, we did not look for an 'empty' to smoke in. None of us smoked, and although we talked of many boyish things, we never talked much about smoking. I think one or two of my friends had had a surreptitious puff in the garden shed or been dared to light up in the bushes on the common, but that was all. We simply did not feel the need to and, if we had, the usual threats from headmasters that any boy found smoking (most heinous of all, in an identifiable school cap) would be caned were enough to deter us. We were, after all, brought up to do as we were told. We respected authority figures in the shape of policemen, officials, teachers, especially headmasters, and we largely obeyed their instructions, especially if they were backed up by the prospect of a good hiding if we did not.

Similarly, we did not swear, even in fun or in irritation. We were told at home and at school not to use swear words and, of course, nothing more than a rare 'damn' or 'blast' was ever heard at home. We were aware of one or two four-letter words used by street urchins and 'rough' boys and, in due course, we showed interest in what they meant but we never dreamed of using them ourselves. Very occasionally at school one heard a 'bloody' but certainly nothing beyond that. I can only remember my father swearing once and I cannot find it in my heart to blame him. We were about to eat our lunch one Sunday in Frederick Place. Just as my father was about to sit down at the table, I pulled his chair away – one of my jokes! He fell backwards onto the floor and cracked his head against the wall. 'You little sod,' he said slowly, while my mother looked on aghast. He did not even hit me, though I deserved it. Yet his, 'Don't you ever do that to me or anyone else again' etched itself on my mind.

We had one little irritating game we used to play on the staff of the refreshment room on Platform I at London Bridge. Outside the door on the wall was a framed tariff and in small print at the bottom was the words: 'Glasses of water may be obtained on request.' One of us would approach the lady at the counter with a smile and say, 'May I have a glass of water, please?' Since this was a quiet time in the afternoon she was happy to oblige. After the third or fourth small boy had come in for a glass of water she was far from happy and threw us out. We played this game intermittently, but regretted it in the summer when we were genuinely hot and were dying for a drink and dared not go in.

Having a season ticket enabled me to travel to certain London termini at weekends, so occasionally I went trainspotting with a friend to Waterloo, Charing Cross or Victoria. I acquired from the library a list, by classes, of the steam engines operating on the Southern Railway and we amused ourselves ticking off the ones we had seen in our notebooks. Visiting the termini gave us access to a wider range of locomotives than those we saw on our daily journeys to and from London Bridge. What is rather surprising is that we went careering all over central London without a thought or frisson of unease. My parents never objected or even saw fit to warn me in coded terms of the minor perils awaiting small boys in major cities. We were perfectly safe in those days.

The steam engines that ran on our part of the Southern Railway belonged to two classes, the 'King Arthur' class and the 'Schools' class. I remember we did Tennyson's *Idylls of the King* early on for English Lit. so I was pretty well up in the doings of the Round Table. When, in due course, I saw *Sir Lancelot*, *Sir Gareth*, *Sir Gawain* and *King Arthur* himself come snorting, ponderous, and clanking into the station, it was like meeting old friends. They looked superb in their green Southern Railway livery, their brass burnished and gleaming in the afternoon sun.

The 'Schools' class of relatively light, compact 4–4–0s was designed for use on routes where the tunnels were too low, the bridges too weak or the gradients too steep for standard 4–6–4. The class of forty engines, built from 1930, was named after famous public schools and I was delighted to find St Olave's had a locomotive named after it. Admittedly it was the thirty-ninth but, still, there it was. How our grammar school (no nonsense about our being a public school – even a minor day one) found itself among the likes of Eton, Harrow, Winchester and Rugby I do not know. Perhaps an Old Olavian, as our old boys were known, had some influence with the Southern Railway or had happened to be on the right committee at the right time. No matter, that was our engine and we all felt a little more significant whenever it took us home.

Outside the brief summer months, stations are cold and draughty places, and London Bridge, being close to the Thames and situated high above the neighbouring streets, was especially bleak in winter. From it, the iron fingers of the Southern Railway stretched out south and south-eastwards into the endless suburbs and the countryside beyond. On the grey, raw afternoons when the fog drifted, smoking in from the river, and the gas lamps flared through the murk, we used to stand on the greasy platform stamping our feet and warming our hands on bags of hot chestnuts. Bags of chestnuts, five for a penny, we bought from the roast-chestnut man who had his little brazier in Tooley Street at the bottom of the station steps.

We used to wait impatiently for the indicator-boards, suspended outside the refreshment room, to light up. Soon afterwards from the loudspeakers in the roof came the disembodied nasal voice, booming up and down the platform. I hear it still. 'The next train on Platform 2 will call at – pause – New Cross, Saint John's, Ladywell, Catford Bridge, Lower Sydenham, New Beckenham, Clockhouse, Elmer's End, Woodside and Addiscombe.' What evocations of *rus in urbe*! Ladywell! Elmer's End! A railway ticket to romantic places a stone's throw from London Bridge. Then came the jolting crash of the signal arms, to be followed by the thunder and hiss of the train as it came snaking, braking, round the curve into the station. How the ghost of it clings!

EIGHTEEN

THE WINE PRESS

'A schoolboy's tale, the wonder of an hour!'

Childe Harold, Byron

Early in September 1938, I returned from my summer holidays, including a fortnight spent at Bognor, to find myself in Upper IVB under the genial eye of Mr Chubb, or 'Chubby'. Our new form room was on the ground floor of the main school, close to the rear entrance to the hall. It was pleasant to find that Lower IVB had moved up en bloc and we were now able to regard the new boys in their unaccustomed collars with some disdain.

In Upper IVB we did not sit in alphabetical order at our double iron-framed desks but were allowed a degree of latitude. I found myself, for a reason I cannot remember, on my own until I was joined a few days after term started by a boy called Noble, who had apparently been ill at the end of the summer holiday. He was, through no fault of his own, an embarrassing classmate. His parents kept a fish and chip shop and his clothes, his hair, every pore of his body was impregnated with the smell of fried fish. It was quite overpowering, so much so that I did most of my work perched precariously at the extreme end of our desk.

We soon settled down. Some subjects were taught by masters new to us and we encountered fresh subjects in Greek, trigonometry and Shakespeare. As the year wore on, I began to realise that I was unresponsive to physics and chemistry and that I was unlikely to excel at either. And while I had always been quick and accurate at arithmetic, I found I was increasingly unable to grasp the concepts of the more advanced algebra and trigonometry I now encountered. However, I did my best and pressed on happily.

At this time, several of us were mad on gym and, as we only had one 'pod' or period a week, we tried to extract as much as possible from it. To cut down the time spent in changing, we started surreptitiously changing into our gym kit during the last ten minutes of the preceding period. We even began to compete with each other in seeing how far we could undress before the bell rang. Gym shoes were easy but our ploy foundered when Carley was spotted fumbling under his desk. Told to stand up, he reluctantly revealed himself without trousers, pants, socks or shoes, clutching his gym shorts protectively in front of him.

Early in the summer term my placid progress was suddenly shattered. I cannot remember being bullied or set upon while I was at Plum Lane; my friendship with the large and powerful Reggie Walker saw to that. I was never bullied nor set upon at Fox Hill either, although I was involved in the usual brief scuffles in the playground and in the street. Despite being accounted clever, I was of average height and keen on games and I had none of those peculiarities, such as glasses, physical deformity, lisp or smell that incite large boys to make the lives of small boys a sickening misery. Nor did I break any taboo or do anything (apart from the incident of the beach shoes) to make me the target of the herd. At home, there was no bully around the block and our gang was luckily left alone by undoubtedly larger lads roaming the neighbourhood. We were always careful in any case when alone, or in twos or threes on the common, and when making our way there and back, to avoid becoming involved with gangs of bigger boys. But I came unstuck at school in a rather curious way.

In Upper IVB I was very friendly with Buggy and we usually travelled up together on the 8.20, sometimes with another boy called Razzell. Raz and I never really liked each other and I was never at ease with him; it was only because he had known Buggy for several years before that we became friendly. He normally travelled from Plumstead, the next station down the line, so he was not really one of us. I saw nothing of him outside school and the Southern Railway while his private life remained a blank. All I knew was that his father was an undertaker and they lived in a flat over the business, which may have accounted for his unusually mordant tongue.

Razzell was thin and spidery with sarcastic eyes that gleamed maliciously (or so I thought) through his pebble glasses, and all this was crowned by a thatch of wavy, red-gold hair. He was inevitably known as 'Razzle' or 'Old Raz', *Razzle* being the title, in those far-off innocent days, of a slightly naughty magazine sold on railway bookstalls. By today's standards it was pretty small beer, but we thought it was smashing.

The actual trouble started during one of those temporary estrangements between Raz and me, which had become more and more frequent. Perhaps he was jealous of my friendship with Buggy. One warm evening in June, I had gone out after tea to play cricket on the common with Buggy and some friends. We played single-wicket stuff until silly mid-off could hardly see the stumps, and then Buggy and I walked slowly homewards across the balding turf. We strolled along Heavitree Road, past pleasant family houses whose back gardens overlooked the tennis courts on the common, turned down Burwash Road and at the bottom on the corner of Durham Road came to Buggy's cosy terrace house, which hardly deserved the name we gave it. Buggy invited me in. I went in for a few incautious minutes. Mrs Bugg offered me a glass of homemade wine. This was life! I was rather partial to homemade wine by then, a result of family visits to Auntie Walters who lived just across the road. Mrs Bugg's wine was sweet and strong, I had had a long day and, after all, I was excitable by nature.

The hot night, running about the common, wine and high spirits combined to produce in me a brittle gaiety that was to be my undoing. It was almost dark when I left the house. Buggy and I said uproarious goodnights; we laughed, we joked – it was all tremendously amusing. And then I ran off down the hill into the night. I went everywhere at the double in those days.

Neither of us had noticed a shape flitting along in the shadows on the opposite side of the road, a slight figure whose glasses glinted in the moonlight, a figure which did not declare its presence but stayed lurking some thirty yards away in the dusk of a draper's doorway. What evil combination of circumstances made old Raz pass Buggy's house at that particular hour that night I shall never know. What he was doing creeping about in the dark so far from home he never mentioned, or had to explain.

Unsuspecting, I caught the 8.20 as usual the next morning. The train was very full and our gang was strung out along the corridor in the rear coach. Razzle was already there. He moved slowly from one boy to another along the corridor, pointing, whispering, miming, insinuating, and it was some minutes before I realised what was happening. Raz had seen all that had happened outside Buggy's house the previous night and he was not the lad to miss a chance like this. Old Bristow had been tipsy last night; he had called at Buggy's house and they had been drinking wine. He had seen old Bristow shouting and singing at the gate – more imitations to the great delight of the corridor. Old Bristow had been drunk; he had seen him, excited, voluble, lurching unsteadily home. The pattern was established and now the delicate embroidery had begun. Not a word, you notice, about Buggy.

In the face of all this, my denials were unconvincing. There was a grain of truth in what old Raz said, but how to convey this to the mob of laughing, exultant faces around me? He kept it up all the way to London Bridge and his invention never flagged. We tumbled out on to the platform and I was swept along and through the barrier and down the steps into Tooley Street. Buggy was very quiet; he had stayed quiet the entire journey. Razzle was far ahead of us along the road, yet I suspected this was the lull before the storm. Surely Raz would not let it stop here? I knew he was up to something, but what exactly his fertile mind had in store for me I could not guess. This was just as well perhaps.

After prayers there were two periods before the mid-morning break. The first was English and this passed safely enough despite Raz's antics. By this time, of course, it was all over the form. Raz was an excellent mimic, and while the master was writing on the blackboard he went rapidly through the various stages of intoxication from the convivial to the paralytic. Several of his cronies, Carley, Crockford and Grant, joined in, with grimaces in my direction, and there was much toasting of imaginary glasses, drinking and swaying about. Harmless enough, you may say.

It was unfortunate that the next period was scripture and we were reading Isaiah. We did that ferocious passage in chapter sixty-three, about the wine press and treading and trampling people down in fury. Rousing stuff, but inopportune, because it was this that suggested to Raz the climax he had been seeking.

The bell went for break and I swarmed out with the others, ears pricked, my whole being alert for the slightest hint of danger. I saw Raz was huddled by the steps with Crockford, Grant and a few others, yet, watchful as I was, they had surrounded me before I could escape, taunting, pushing, yelling, 'Drunk! Drunk! Drunk!' Raz, Svengali-like in the background, played upon their simple boyish passions. Then, suddenly, there he was, in the front, in command, shouting, 'He's full of wine, he's full of wine. We must squeeze him dry. To the wine press with him.' The cry, 'To the wine press!' was taken up by the crowd which had now grown to about twenty. 'The wine press, the wine press', they chanted, and I was borne struggling to a corner of the playground – a very special corner.

Our playground was large but irregular. In one corner, almost joining the corner of the small new block were two fives courts, and between the side wall of the courts and the main fabric was a narrow passage. As it led to a tiny playground used by the two prep. forms, it was blocked off halfway along by a strong wooden partition some 6ft high, thus forming a tiny, cul-de-sac, an appendix some 10ft long by 3ft wide, with brick walls on either side. That partition is crystal-clear in my mind. It was made of vertical planking fixed to stout horizontal beams, and at the bottom the planks were beginning to splinter under the impact of a thousand idle toecaps. It was an obscure place and, until that fateful morning, used for furtive conversations and the more secretive sorts of schoolboy pursuits.

I was carried to the mouth of this passage, bundled roughly into it, and jammed against the partition by two of the heaviest boys in the class. Yelling form mates closed in after them, more piled in behind and the passage became a seething jumble of the principal parts of boy. The pressure built up, a rhythmical shove developed and the crowd swayed forwards and backwards to cries of 'Heave! Heave!' I was spread-eagled across the partition, pinned like a butterfly on a board, with the horizontal beams biting into my chest and thighs. More boys, attracted by the din, ran up, hoping, as always, to see a fight. What they saw was something much more subtle. Old Raz, wily general that he was, now led his men from behind. Seeing reinforcements approaching, he shouted, 'He's full of wine. We're pressing it out.' There was a general cry of 'It's the wine press, it's the wine press!' And in that painful moment a tradition was born.

I was saved by the bell; I have never heard a more welcome sound. The unbearable pressure suddenly eased, as the crowd behind me melted away and I slumped backwards, white-faced and panting.

At dinnertime, boys being boys, the punishment was repeated. I was found skulking in a corner of the playground and again there were Raz-inspired shouts of, 'To the wine press!' Once more they carried me, protesting and struggling, to that evil little cul-de-sac in the corner of the playground. Practice makes perfect and this time the treatment was even more effective, quite terrifying, in fact, and once more I dragged myself, bruised, sore and shaking, back to the form room. Yet, boys being boys, my ordeal stopped that day and was never repeated, despite frantic efforts by Raz to whip up feeling against me. Schoolboys have an instinctive sense of the fitness of things; justice was swift, justice was certainly rough, but they considered I had had enough. I had, too, I most certainly had.

The wine press was not forgotten. From that day onwards anyone in our form (and it soon spread to the other forms) who had offended the class or transgressed the code was whirled away to the corner near the fives courts, there to be ground, crushed and squeezed to a palpitating pulp. In a few weeks the wine press became the most popular form of punishment, yet it was to be short-lived. A few months later the war broke out and our school was evacuated. By the time the school returned, the partition had disappeared, links with the past had been broken, certain traditions had faded and, as far as the wine press was concerned, there was no race memory. I find this faintly disappointing. I should like to have gone down in the annals of Stogs as the boy responsible for the punishment of the wine press.

NINETEEN

GROWING PAINS

'Children begin by loving their parents; after a time, they
judge them; rarely, if ever, do they forgive them.'
A Woman of No Importance, Oscar Wilde

Despite the unpleasantness of the wine press I was happy during the
years I spent at St Olave's. The wine press incident turned out to
be an isolated one and I was never ragged or bullied any more. In
a way, the affair did me some good by establishing a kind of persona for
me. The spurious glamour attached to 'drink' hung round me and made
me stand out a little from the pack.

We were very well taught, of that there is no question, and I thrived in
the competitive academic atmosphere. I had received a solid foundation at
Foxhill and now the masters at St Olave's built on that. I took to the
grammar-school curriculum like a duck to water. Latin and French were
new subjects to me, as were physics and chemistry; history and geography
were familiar but were now much more ordered, one into periods and the
other into regions. There was much emphasis, as you might expect, upon
English, formal grammar, composition and literature. The rigour of this
timetable was tempered by double periods of art and woodwork, and a
gym period. The curriculum was certainly not sullied by anything remotely
smacking of relevance, current affairs or social studies.

Like most able children, I was a sponge, soaking up strange languages, facts
and figures, theories and theorems, to be regularly squeezed out of me in
minor tests and major end-of-term and annual examinations. This monkey-
like ability to absorb and retain was further developed at St Olave's by
learning poetry by heart, by learning vocabulary lists, lists of principal parts,
strings of dates, the conjugation of Latin and French verbs, the declension of
nouns and passages from Shakespeare. It all went in at both ears and stayed
in; my powers of memory were thus strengthened, flexed and tested.

Naturally, some subjects appeared to us to be taught more sympathetically
than others. For example, we had a gifted and imaginative young master

called Smith, who taught us French. This was not yet the era of direct method but he put much emphasis on pronunciation drills and grammar, and his lessons were always laced with French songs (he had a pleasing tenor voice) or spelling bees or word games. He gave those of us with a quick ear the beginnings of an accent that was not Stratford-atte-Bowe.

I dimly began to realise that the time devoted to English grammar – parsing, clause analysis et al. – accompanied and underpinned a thorough grounding in Latin, French and, later, Greek. If I have a criticism to make about the teaching of one or two subjects, it is of a certain lack of imagination. I found the teaching of English uninspired and uninspiring with few sparks being kindled in the literature periods. But I am most grateful for being taught that demanding and elegant exercise, the art of précis. The fact that we were close to the Thames, a stone's throw from Tower Bridge and within bowshot of the Tower of London, surrounded by the evidence, liquid and otherwise, of 2,000 years of history, seemed to have no impact on the teaching of English, History or Latin. Shakespeare was set before us, without preamble, simply as a text, with no attempt to place him in the context of Elizabethan England or to prepare us for his language. Yet Bankside and the site of the Globe Theatre itself were only a little way beyond London Bridge station. And I am far from convinced that *A Midsummer Night's Dream* is the ideal introduction for small boys, despite Bottom and the rustics.

It is difficult to teach English literature or even European history badly to intelligent boys. It is also difficult to imagine any period of our history which is not dominated by London. Yet, although Traitor's Gate grinned at us across the river, we were never taken to the Tower, to St Paul's, the Monument or to the Houses of Parliament. I cannot remember even being specifically recommended to visit these, or any other places, or the London museums either. It was lucky that so many of us had thoughtful parents. Again, Latin was taught most thoroughly but with no reference to Londinium across the water, and no suggestion of visiting Roman remains there or elsewhere. As for art, we used to troop up to the light and airy studio at the top of the new classroom block from which there were splendid views of the city skyline and the river. All I ever remember drawing is buckets, varied occasionally by painting 'My impression of Bonfire Night'. We were never encouraged to look (indeed, looking out of the windows, in art as in other subjects, was actively discouraged), to sketch, to learn to see, or to examine buildings. I was hopeless at art in any case.

Regular homework to supplement our class work was set from the outset and I rapidly became accustomed to working on my own. Homework was always meticulously marked or tested – and, naturally, recorded. Thus I fell into a daily routine of travelling, class work and homework during the school year, which was to continue until it was rudely interrupted by the war in 1939.

For us worms at the bottom of the heap, life was earnest, life was real. We were driven hard, tested and tried at every turn, but we thrived on it and I began to forge ahead. St Olave's was regarded as a crack school which, within its restricted terms of reference – successes in school certificate and matriculation, higher school certificate, and scholarships and exhibitions to Oxford and Cambridge – it certainly was.

Being situated on the South Bank, St Olave's obviously had no playing fields adjoining it; in fact, there was not a blade of grass in sight for miles. Our playing fields were at East Dulwich and that is where we travelled on Saturday mornings for cricket and football. For me, like most of the others, it meant an extra train journey. I had to go to London Bridge, cross to the other part of the station, catch a train to East Dulwich and walk a short way to our grounds. I accepted this naturally and unhesitatingly as part of the pattern that was being woven for me. I enjoyed the cricket particularly, because I was keen as mustard and had the makings of a useful batsman. Football was a different matter. Although I had played for years with my friends, I was not very good at it and I eventually settled for becoming a goalkeeper. I was not particularly brilliant at that either but I chose that position, I suppose, because it had a certain theatrical quality. Racing out of my goal to clear or diving at the feet of an opposing forward made me feel like an embryonic Sam Bartram, a feeling not always shared by my teammates. I remember, with shame, the dying moments of a closely-fought house match when, with the teams level, I attempted to clear a muddy ball near the post and managed to throw it through my own goal. I also developed into quite a useful sprinter but came face to face with reality at my first annual sports day when, more out of bravado than anything else, I entered for the quarter mile. I managed to finish about eighth out of twelve, but I was so dizzy and exhausted and my chest was heaving so painfully that I never ventured beyond a hundred yards again.

When I passed the scholarship examination and went to St Olave's, I became the first generation grammar school child *par excellence*. As the months went by, I found that the nature of the work I was doing was beginning to draw me away from my parents. I was bound for regions where they could not follow. They smiled indulgently and in amused puzzlement over my homework in Latin, chemistry and French and wondered aloud where it would all lead. It would lead, in due course, to my emotional estrangement from them in adolescence and my uprooting from my background. To be fair, I do not think I realised what was happening to me, and if I had (a tall order for a boy of twelve or thirteen), I do not think I would have had the insight and sympathetic understanding to have dealt with it. It is hard being clever but not very intelligent.

In his book, *The Uses of Literacy*, Richard Hoggart has a brilliant but uncomfortable chapter entitled 'Unbent Springs: A Note on the Uprooted and Anxious'. Although my background was not gregarious working-class, there are considerable similarities with the problems exposed and discussed by Hoggart. In my own case, the problems of the able child being educated out of his class and becoming divorced from his family and environment were exacerbated by my being an only child. When I was thirteen I dimly realised that a gap was opening up between my parents and me, but I had not yet reached the stage of being embarrassed by my father on some social occasions, of being contemptuous of my parents' tastes, and critical of their attitudes. That painful period of agonising and self-torment was to come a few years later and lies, fortunately for my *amour propre*, outside the scope of this story of childhood. Being a bright only child had all the classic effects upon my personality and character you would expect. Away from my academic womb I was painfully shy and self-conscious, a potential loner; I was, not unnaturally, self-centred and, sadly, inclined to be selfish, mainly because I rarely had to share anything with anybody. Such handicaps, steadily reinforced by regular academic success, are not lightly overcome in later life.

These problems, however, were below the horizon in the two years before the war. If I have to pinpoint the sharpest, most evocative memory of that period at St Olave's, it would be of those Friday afternoons in winter when we used to assemble in the hall for prayers and dismissal at half-past three. All the potent magic of my schooldays is concentrated on that scene on November afternoons when the grey dank day was nearly done and a thin fog began to rise from the river. It crept across the wharves and warehouses on the South Bank, swirled round the dingy tenements of Tooley Street, and insinuated itself through the doors and windows of the school. The electric chandeliers were on as we filed into our cavernous hall and already the white tunnel arching high above our heads was dim in their misty glow. As we shuffled into position, we could taste the fog, sulphurous, Dickensian. We stood in silence. A pause. The head entered, mounted the platform, and announced, 'Hymn 283. Two, eight, three. "Immortal, Invisible".' It was always 'Immortal, Invisible', or so it seemed, on those winter afternoons in the dusk.

We opened our school hymn books. I can feel the texture of mine still; my mother covered it in black hopsack, a cloth that grew shinier and shinier as the terms slowly passed. Number 283. In his nest high above us and barely visible in the gloom, Mr Cramp sat poised at the organ, his head and shoulders outlined by the small light above the keyboard.

A pause. Then the organ crashed out, shattering the stillness. 'Immortal, invisible, God only wise.' I glanced up through the windows at the darkening sky. A yellow light fell on the fading garlands on the war memorial. 'Almighty, victorious, Thy great name we praise.' From the wall panels our predecessors' names and achievements shone fitfully but encouragingly down at us. Behind me the sound swelled as the power was unleashed by the fifth and sixth forms:

> 'We blossom and flourish as leaves on the tree,
> And wither and perish; but naught changeth thee.'

Golden lads . . . golden futures.

Through the thickening fog came the distant trumpeting of tugs on London river and the long, slow, sad trombone from some lone freighter in the pool. 'All laud we would render; O help us to see' – the school braced itself for the climax – ''Tis only the splendour of light hideth Thee.' A great hush. The last organ notes still vibrated in our ears. We bowed our heads. The blessing. A cough at the back of the hall in the silence. 'The love of God and the fellowship of the Holy Spirit be with us all evermore. Amen.'

Amen, I say to all that. Amen.

TWENTY

THE END
OF THE BEGINNING

'"It's a poor sort of memory that only works backwards," the
Queen remarked.'

Through the Looking-Glass, Lewis Carroll

In the summer of 1939 my father, greatly daring, took us to Belgium for
our first foreign holiday. I can only marvel at his bravado since neither
he nor my mother spoke a word of French apart from such jocular
phrases as '*oui oui, san ferry ann, voulez-vous promener avec moi,
mamselle? bonjour,* and *pommes de terre.*' This was hardly a promising
vocabulary with which to confront the natives. None of my friends at
school or any of our relatives had ever been across the Channel, except
those who, like Uncle Jim and my father, had gone at King George's
expense. So one morning in early August, with a carefree disregard for the
possibility of war, we caught the ferry at Dover and set off for a fortnight
in Ostend.

We stayed in the Nelson Hotel, a small 'English' hotel in the Rue
Louise, one of the cobbled streets leading down to the promenade, not far
from the Kursaal. This was another first, for we had never stayed in a
proper hotel together before. I managed to eat enough of the unfamiliar
food to sustain life, but I did not care for the combined odours of garlic
and cooking oil wafting up from the basement kitchens on our way to the
sea front. 'It turns my stomach over', said my mother.

We spent much of our time on the beach, punctuated by coach trips to
places of interest. Once we grasped that the various Belgians we met
understood English, if spoken slowly and loudly, life became less stressful.
On the strength of my having done French for two years at St Olave's, my
parents, much to my embarrassment, kept ushering me forward as
situations presented themselves, to say something in French. I quickly
realised that with a small vocabulary, little grammar and no confidence,

By sea to Ostend.

and with none of the emollient expressions of the phrase book at my command, I was going to be neither use nor ornament – and what's the French for that, I wondered? Disaster finally overtook me while we were on a trip to Paris Plage, or Le Touquet. Being a keen stamp collector I made my way to the post office and, when I reached the head of the queue, asked carefully and politely for two forty-centime stamps. I stared in disbelief as the clerk tore off half a page of two-centime stamps and handed me forty. I was suddenly struck dumb, overcome with confusion, unable to utter even one word from my limited stock. Fortunately, an Englishman in the queue took pity on me and explained my predicament in fluent French. Within seconds, clutching my two stamps in a moist palm, I was slinking out of the bureau de poste, pink-faced and ashamed, feeling the eyes of all France were upon me.

Apart from this incident, the holiday was a great success. Besides Le Touquet and the lovely old city of Bruges, we went to Zeebrugge not far away up the coast to look at the mole and the memorial to those who were killed in the gallant action to deny the harbour to German submarines on St George's Day, 1918. For me, however, the most exciting trip was the tour of the Flanders battlefields. Our coach took us first to Ypres and then, starting from the Menin Gate, we saw Hellfire Corner,

With Father at Vimy Ridge.

visited Hill 60, and ended up at the impressive Canadian memorial on Vimy Ridge. I have a snap of myself, correctly dressed in blazer, grey shorts and school cap, standing with my father by preserved trenches of the Canadian front line. (I have another one of myself, this time casually dressed, standing in exactly the same spot nearly fifty years later). We also crossed the Scheldt to go to Middelbergh so I was able to boast to my friends on my return that I had been to Belgium, France and Holland.

Back in London the holiday mood soon dissipated amid rumours of war. My parents listened anxiously to the six o'clock news and wondered what the future held in store for us. Sombrely we collected our gas masks in their cardboard carrying cases. I still went up to the common on those hot summer evenings and played cricket and messed about in the street, but it became apparent even to me that the next September term was not to be the start of an ordinary school year.

There was talk on the wireless and articles in the newspapers about plans for the evacuation of children from London and the major industrial cities. Since St Olave's was opposite the Tower and the City, smack among the docks and wharves of London river, my parents reckoned we were bound to be high on the priority list for evacuation if war broke out. I remained happily unconcerned at the prospect. Then, towards the end of August, my father received a letter from Dr Carrington detailing what we had to bring with us at the start of term in case it was decided to evacuate the school at short notice.

So the first day of term saw us staggering up to London Bridge loaded with suitcases, kitbags, mackintoshes, and with our gas masks slung across our backs. A few boys even carried bulky parcels tied up with hairy string, but this was frowned upon by Dr Carrington who had quite clearly forbidden parcels in his instructions. Boys at Stogs, like guards officers, did not carry parcels. When we arrived at school we were told, sensibly, to return to our old form rooms and form masters until further notice, so we stacked our luggage round the sides of our familiar room and settled down with Chubby to wait for war. When it failed to materialise, we went home minus baggage at the end of the afternoon, returning the next morning impatient for the off. The outbreak of war was imminent now and I knew that my move into Lower VA would not take place at St Olave's in Tooley Street.

This waiting, this suspension of normal school activity, went on for a couple of days. Boys are insensitive little beasts and we all thought it was a marvellous adventure. It only fitfully crossed our minds that we were about to be torn from the bosom of our family, taken to an unknown destination and there thrust into the bosom of someone else's. But we took all this in our stride. For one thing, we had a marvellous time at school. There was no attempt at formal lessons; it was like that happy time in midsummer when the examinations are over, the staff are up to their eyes in marking and it's, 'Reading books out', or quiet games. Our old form master, burly, reassuring, pipe-smoking Chubby, understood small boys. He read to us for hours and we played variations on the usual word games round the class. When we tired of this, he split us up into small groups and then moved from group to group, teaching us how to play bridge and improving our chess. We read, talked, drew, played hangman and battleships and the less respectable card games – and authority smiled upon us.

The order to move came early on the morning of Friday 1 September, soon after we had arrived once again from home. We extracted our luggage, lugged it outside and found the whole school assembling in the playground. Form by form we moved off round the back of the school and out through the main gates into Tooley Street. I did not realise it then, but it was to be the last time I would pass through that entrance.

The September sun was hot on our backs as we sweated with our luggage towards London Bridge station. The inhabitants had never seen a procession like this before and their comments were loud, pithy and pointed as the immense crocodile passed unsteadily along Tooley Street. At least we were spared the indignity of having luggage labels tied to our lapels bearing name, school and next of kin. I was lugging a suitcase and I soon began to envy those few boys who were carrying kitbags, which proved so much more manoeuvrable. My friend Buggy had a new snow-white kitbag on which his father, an old army man, had printed his surname in large, black block letters. He then added his son's initial; it was a pity they had christened him simply 'Ralph'. Buggy had managed to hide this inscription on our way along Tooley Street but he met his Waterloo, if I may put it like that, at London Bridge station. As he swung along the platform, his name could be read thirty yards away. The porters were in their element. Cries of, 'Come on, you young bugger!', 'Step it out, you poor old bugger!' and 'Bugger me, what a sight!' rang out across the platforms. We were all rather embarrassed for him.

We lined up along the platform, an empty train came curving in from Charing Cross and we all piled aboard. Half an hour later, after careful checking and re-checking of lists of boys by the staff, there was a shrill blast from the engine and we puffed off into the unknown. There were no tears shed at our departure, no handkerchiefs fluttered for us, no affectionate arms waved until we were out of sight, for our parents were scattered all over south-east London. They had no idea we were being evacuated that morning and naturally had no knowledge of where we were going. I think the staff knew but they were unusually sphinx-like about it. Inside the crowded compartment we were tremendously excited. To what romantic spot, to what resort of infinite possibilities for small boys were we bound? Visions of endless delight by land and sea filled our heads. It turned out to be Uckfield. The very name is like a bell. Uckfield!

This brief journey into the Sussex countryside was to signal the end of boyhood. As I peered out of the window at the familiar vista of endless streets and shabby buildings, the train carried me away from that small part of London to which I should never return. I sank back into my seat as a new life opened out before me.

EPILOGUE

'Autobiography can be the laying to rest of ghosts, as well as an ordering of the mind.'

Writing Autobiography, Laurie Lee

If, gentle reader, you have struggled thus far, I thought I might persuade you to read one more chapter, even though my own story has ended. I have always enjoyed that last chapter in many Victorian novels in which, after the climax and resolution of the drama, the author describes what happened to the principal characters in later years. He details who married whom, how many children they produced, where they lived and their progress through life. This is an unpopular technique with contemporary novelists but I think it still gives a rounding-off, a satisfying sense of completion, to a narrative.

As we have seen, I left Woolwich in September 1939 and never returned to live there. I rarely visited it afterwards because I had no friends left in the area, either from Fox Hill or from my St Olave's days – we had all been *déraciné* by the war. The only reason for my going back was to see members of the Burrage Road Bristows, who by this time had moved up to Shooter's Hill, and even I lost touch with them for long periods. Since I did, however, pay several visits to my old haunts in the early 1980s, I thought that a few observations on the changes and havoc wrought by time might be of some interest, as also might be comments on a few of the characters who have appeared briefly in my story. Only a few, because nearly all those mentioned are dead and the details of their unremarkable lives can hold little interest for you.

Of all that array of aunts and uncles on my father's side, I am the only living male descendant. My cousin, Alan, Uncle George's only son, was killed in 1942 in North Africa serving in the RAF. So, as I have only managed to father three daughters, the name dies with me, the last of the Bristows. Jim died a little prematurely, but hardly surprisingly, in 1963. If there is a dustcart in heaven being driven round the fields of asphodel collecting up the empty cans of ambrosia, then Jim will be at the wheel, smiling his beatific smile. Of my mother's family, none is left. Her youngest sister, Dot, an active Christian who with her vigour, spirit and cheerfulness proved an example to us all, died in her nineties only a few years ago.

Of the Burrage Road Bristows, only Peter, now well into his eighties, survives and the years sit lightly upon him. His brother, Eric, went to join the Great Scorer in 1987, aged seventy-six, and in his will left me his collection of cricket books. This contained a quantity of *Wisdens*, a fifty-three-year run of bound volumes of *The Cricketer* from 1927 to 1979, plus many general cricket books. I cannot think of a more thoughtful and delightful legacy. When I grow even older, I shall draw my chair up nearer the fire, pull my shawl closer round my shoulders, take up a treasured volume and lose myself in memories of those sunlit days of the 1930s.

I did not see Stan for many years but I met him again when he began to pay what became an annual visit to my parents, who by this time were living at St Leonards-on-Sea. When Stan first started coming down from Ilford to see them they looked forward to his visits since they had been friends since the beginning of the 1920s. Sadly, they began to consider him a bore ('We've heard all his stories so many times') and then as something of a nuisance, someone who had to be accommodated. My wife and I savoured his company and thought him pure gold. Life had not treated him well; his wife, to whom he was devoted, became mentally ill and was in and out of institutions until her death. He never remarried, but always remained uncomplaining and amusing in company before returning to what must have been a cheerless and lonely house. Fortunately, his old age was sweetened by a new hearing aid so that at long last he could listen comfortably to his favourite pieces of music.

In his retirement, nothing gave Stan greater pleasure than to visit one of the Essex county grounds and sit with his friends outside the pavilion chatting about the heroes of the past and the more inscrutable decisions of the present committee. Stan's vivid turn of phrase would debar him from the pavilion in the Elysian Fields but I am sure he will be found sitting on a bench on the boundary, nodding and smiling and making his point by tapping the knee of his angelic neighbour, Eric.

I find it poignant that all those men and women who taught me at school and my various lecturers at Cambridge, their faces still so clearly etched in my memory, their personalities and quirks of character so vividly remembered, are now dead. Cyril Bull, I discovered, died in 1963, aged sixty-nine, and his obituary notice commented that 'he gave his life to the service of others and both young and old have equal cause to remember his kindness.' A fitting testimonial, indeed.

And what of the area? Woolwich and Plumstead, like most outer suburbs of London, suffered much from bombing during the war, though the damage was mainly confined to the lower part of the town. War damage and the blight of the post-war years combined to produce that aura of seediness and dereliction common to so much of south and south-east London. This atmosphere has not been helped in recent years by extensive redevelopment and the building of unsympathetic blocks of flats and houses. The composition of the population has also changed, for there is now a significant immigrant community. In fact, ethnically, the area resembles a pyramid with a coloured base which grows steadily lighter as one moves uphill through Plumstead until one emerges onto the white highlands of Shooter's Hill.

Even so, I cannot get over the fact that after so many years the small area in which I spent my boyhood has altered so little, despite the ravages of war. Subconsciously, I imagine I expected that half a century and more would have wrought vast changes. Certainly, much seemed dirtier and uncared for, yet, by and large, it was immediately recognisable. I suppose it was because I lived in a mature residential district where there were no fields to be obliterated by housing or industrial estates and where the open spaces were jealously preserved.

The shops along Plumstead Common Road and Herbert Road look run-down and impoverished, which is true of most shops in the area outside the new pedestrianised precincts of Powis Street and Hare Street. Beresford Square seems as lively as ever, presided over by the imposing entrance to the Arsenal, but the dockyard is no more and most of the Arsenal has been demolished. The approaches to the Free Ferry have been so re-developed as to be unrecognisable but the Granada and the Odeon (now the Coronet) are still there, though no longer quite the proud picture palaces of the past.

Strangely, the three houses in which I lived, in Tuam Road, Herbert Road and Frederick Place, all escaped damage. The first and last of these terrace houses now look very trim and smart, though it is difficult to see them clearly and whole because of the continuous lines of parked cars. Frederick Place itself and the block are little changed although the Freemasons Arms is now the Bag of Nails and the old Co-op building houses a colourful tile centre. But the triangle in Conduit Road, where Derek Sargent used to live, has been demolished and there is no trace of the Baptist chapel. For old time's sake, I walked back from Plumstead Common down Burwash Road to have a look at Auntie Walter's house in Durham Road (now Durham Rise); it was still there and so was Buggy's on the opposite corner. I continued down Durham Road and then was suddenly and utterly lost; the whole area around Raglan Road had been redeveloped. Roads I knew had disappeared, Meckiff's shop had gone and I could find nothing familiar in the moonscape facing me. I felt uneasy and was glad to hasten away.

As far as the army presence is concerned, much remains in good order. The Military Academy and the great Royal Artillery barracks and parade ground are still most impressive, while the Rotunda Museum is as splendid as ever. The Garrison church was destroyed by a flying bomb in 1944; part of the apse and many memorials survived and the ruins now form a garden, a quiet refuge from the traffic thundering along the main road outside. The Royal Artillery Theatre survived the war but was eventually closed in 1954.

Of the parks and commons of my boyhood, Eaglesfield and Shrewsbury Parks and the woods on the shoulder of Shooter's Hill remain remarkably untouched by the years and appear well cared for. The undergrowth in Shrewsbury Park is not nearly as thick as memory insists it was, and my gnarled and polished old climbing tree is no more. Gone, too, is the tennis club which Buggy and I once haunted.

Plumstead Common, although the same in outline, has suffered considerably in detail. Fishbone Alley and its railings have disappeared, although the artillery memorial still stands at the top of the slope, while the Globe cinema has been demolished and replaced by a small block of flats. Most painful of all, the bandstand has disappeared and the immediate area has been surrounded by an ugly palisade, consisting of a high wooden fence, decorated by graffiti, supported by concrete posts and topped by barbed wire, to form the Plumstead adventure playground for the 5–6s. Inside the perimeter are a number of painted wooden structures for the children and a large prefab. It is not a pretty sight.

For there are ghosts here, spirits of the crowds who sauntered across the common on warm summer evenings before the war and listened to the band. If those same ghosts floated up past the tennis courts and bowling greens, over the road to the cricket ground, they would weep invisible tears. The pavilion is dilapidated and the two public houses nearby seem to have fallen on hard times. When I walked across the rough and unloved turf where Eric, my father and I had all played in our various teams long ago, I looked in vain for traces of a square. Alas, the ground had been marked out as a gridiron for American football.

I went back to see my two old schools and my spirits lifted. I did not go inside Plum Lane (now Plumcroft Primary School) but externally it looked just the same. I did go, however, into Fox Hill which is no longer a school but is used for various adult education purposes. It was uncanny to walk into my former junior school for the first time in over fifty years and find it virtually untouched by time. True, the hall had lost its dais and the photographs of the scholarship boys had been swept from the walls long ago, but it was instinct with the personality of Cyril Bull. I looked into the old classrooms; even the open fireplace in Mr Codrington's room was still in place, though hidden behind a large storage heater. I walked through the cloakrooms and out into the playground to find the outside lavatories still intact, as was the wall against which we once played cigarette cards. The school had been recently redecorated and, like so many solid buildings of its era, looked good for another hundred years.

I also visited St Olave's a little while ago. At London Bridge I went down the steps into Tooley Street and was amazed at the transformation that was taking place along the left-hand side between the road and the river. By courtesy of Laing and London Demolition, the giant warehouses were being razed to the ground; some were still standing, their dark carcasses irregularly sliced through to expose light-coloured intestines. The scene resembled Rome sacked by the Goths or the aftermath of some monstrous air raid. I was reassured to find St Olave's apparently untouched by the war and looking as I had first seen it in 1937. It is now, I understand, a listed building. The school had moved out to new premises in Orpington in 1967 and the buildings now formed the Tower Bridge branch of the South London College. I met the head of department in charge in Dr Carrington's old room. I had only been inside it once before – on that unforgettable occasion – but now, seen in tranquillity and not in stomach-churning panic, it struck me as handsome a study as the most imposing headmaster could desire.

I wandered round to the back and found the playground unchanged, except that the fives courts had been demolished and that there was no trace, of course, of the infamous wine press. Inside, however, it was a different matter. The main building now housed a variety of science courses and there had been much partitioning and alteration to create new laboratories and workrooms. As classes were in session I could only look round discreetly. The hall looked particularly bare; gone were the organ and the war memorial, and gone, too, the oak panels recording the successes of the pre-war Oxbridge undergraduates. These panels, I understand, disappeared soon after the move to Orpington and were never found. I looked for my old form room (Upper IVB), where we had waited with our cases for evacuation, and found it had been altered to form part of a kitchen area and staff canteen. Shades of Chubby!

Sadly I left the building and, with wandering steps and slow, down Tooley Street I took my solitary way.